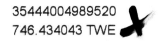

Daisy Farm Crafts

25 CROCHET BABY BLANKET PATTERNS

25 CROCHET BABY BLANKET PATTERNS

By Daisy Farm Crafts

Patterns by Tiffany Brown, Hannah Brown McKay, Nicolina Brown, Haley Brown and Annie Brown

ISBN: 9798649143844

CONTENT

ABBREVIATIONS

YO - Yarn Over

CH - Chain

ST - Stitch

SK - Skip

REP - Repeat

SL ST - Slip Stitch

SC - Single Crochet

HDC - Half Double Crochet

WHDC - Wide Half Double Crochet

HHDC - Herringbone Half Double Crochet

HBDC - Herringbone Double Crochet

DC - Double Crochet

FP/BP - Front Post/Back Post

CL - Cluster

CROCHET TIPS

CHANGING COLORS: When it is time to add in a new color, work to the very last step of the stitch. Before pulling through and finishing the stitch, lay the new color across the hook and pull through with the new color. Cut the old color leaving about a 9 inch tail to weave in later. Begin crocheting with the new color.

WEAVING IN ENDS: When you are finished with the entire blanket you will use a tapestry needle to thread the yarn in and out any of the stitches that are the same color. Weave in and out several times to secure the ends. Cut the tail close to the blanket and the end will disappear into the blanket.

PRACTICE SWATCHES: It's always a good idea to make a small practice swatch before you start your blanket to make sure you understand the stitches and to make sure you are using the right hook size for your personal tension. This is also referred to as checking your gauge.

CARRYING YARN: Carrying yarn is a technique we use to easily change colors in the same row. When carrying yarn, lay the color not in use across the top of your work and crochet over it as you go. The best way to keep your yarn from getting twisted is to always keep one color to the front of your work and one color to the back of your work each time you change colors.

BLOCKING YOUR BLANKET: If you'd like to add finishing touches to your blanket, lay it out flat on a towel or foam blocking boards if you have them. Use a spray bottle with water to dampen the blanket. Press the blanket into straight lines, massaging the stitches and adjusting your tension. Pin with straight pins to let it dry.

Visit the Daisy Farm Crafts YouTube Channel for free crochet video tutorials!

PINK GINGHAM BABY BLANKET

By Tiffany

MATERIALS

YARN   Caron Simply Soft
         (100% acrylic, 170 g/6 oz, 288 m/315 yds)
         3 balls White
         3 balls Soft Pink
         2 balls Strawberry

HOOK   Size H, 5.00mm hook or
         Size I, 5.50mm or
         Size J, 6.00mm hook

TOOLS   Tapestry needle, Scissors

SIZE   Finished size: 36 in x 36 in
         Gauge: 4 in = 16 stitches and 12 rows

STITCHES

SINGLE CROCHET (SC): Insert your hook, yarn over (YO) and pull up a loop, YO, pull through two loops.

SLIP STITCH (SL ST): Insert your hook, YO and pull up a loop and pull directly through loops on hook.

PATTERN

CHAIN 131 with Soft Pink. (Pattern repeat is any odd number multiplied by 10, plus one.)

Tip: I encourage you to make a practice swatch before beginning this blanket. You will want to make sure you use the proper hook size. If it's too small your gingham blanket will be tight like a rug; if it's too big, the yarn being carried may show through too much. Some carried yarn will peek through; this is normal and adds to the gingham look.

ROW 1: SC into the 2nd chain from the hook. Work 1 SC into each of the next 9 chains, pulling through with White on the 10th SC. Work 1 SC with White into each of the next 10 chains, laying the Soft Pink across the chain and crocheting over it as you work.
Be sure and keep the yarn being carried along the row somewhat taut. On the last step of the 10th stitch, pull through with Soft Pink and SC in the next 10 chains, crocheting over the White. Continue alternating the colors every 10 chains, crocheting over the yarn not in use, and pulling through with the new color on the 10th stitch. CH 1 and turn.

ROWS 2 - 10: Wrap the White around the end of your work and continue to single crochet over it and carry the tail along for the first 10 stitches of Soft Pink, then pull through with White on the 10th stitch as before. Continue switching colors every 10 stitches, always crocheting over whichever color isn't in use. Always CH 1 and turn.

ROWS 11 - 20: At the end of your 10th row, cut off the White. SC in each of the first 10 stitches with Strawberry, then on the 10th SC, pull through with Soft Pink. Continue as before, alternating the colors every 10 stitches. Soft Pink should be worked into the White and Strawberry should be worked into Soft Pink on row 11. Always CH 1 and turn after each row.

REPEAT ROWS 2 - 20 UNTIL YOU HAVE 130 ROWS. Tie off and weave in all ends before you begin the border.

Tip: To avoid your yarn getting twisted as you carry it along your work, keep one color to the back of your work and one color to the front of your work each time you change colors.

BORDER

ROUND 1: With White, pull up a loop in any corner of the blanket. SC into each stitch and work 1 SC into the end of each row around the entire blanket, working 3 SC into each corner. Do not join.

Tip: If the sides of your blanket appear fanned out, try changing to a smaller hook, or if the sides of your blanket look gathered, try a larger hook.

ROUND 2: Continuing on in the same direction, SC in the next stitch. *CH 5, slip stitch around the post of the SC you just made making a loop. SC into the next 4 stitches. Repeat from * all the way around. If you happen to be working around a corner, work 2 SC into the corner SC. Slip stitch to join the round.

ROUND 3: Continuing on in the same direction, *6 SC around the circle of chains. Skip over the next SC, SC into the next 2 stitches, skip the next SC. Continue repeating from *around the whole blanket.

ROUND 4: Continuing on in the same direction, SC into each and every stitch. Slip stitch when you get to the stitch you started with and fasten off. Weave in the ends with a tapestry needle.

TEAL STRIPES BABY BLANKET

By Hannah

MATERIALS

YARN   Paton's Canadiana
(100% acrylic, 100 g/3.5 oz, 187 m 205 yds)
4 skeins White
1 skein Pale Teal
1 skein Medium Teal
1 skein Teal Heather

HOOK   Size H, 5.00mm hook

TOOLS   Tapestry needle, Scissors

SIZE   Finished size: 30 in x 36 in
Gauge: 4 in = 15 stitches and 16 rows

STITCHES

SINGLE CROCHET (SC): Insert your hook, yarn over (YO) and pull up a loop, YO and pull through both loops on your hook.

HERRINGBONE HALF DOUBLE CROCHET (HHDC): YO, insert your hook, YO, pull up a loop and pull directly through the first loop on your hook. YO and pull through both loops on your hook.

DOUBLE CROCHET (DC): YO, insert your hook, YO, pull up a loop, YO, pull through two loops, YO, pull through remaining two loops on your hook.

FRONT AND BACK POST DOUBLE CROCHET (FPDC & BPDC): A front post double crochet means you insert your hook from front to back around the post of the next DC and work a DC. A back post double crochet means you insert your hook from back to front around the post of the next DC and work a DC.

PATTERN

CHAIN 110 (or any number) with White.

ROW 1: Starting in the 3rd chain from the hook, work 1 HHDC. Work 1 HHDC into each chain across. CH 2 and turn. (108 HHDC)

ROW 2: Work 1 HHDC in each stitch across the row. On the last stitch of the row, pull through with Teal. (*You should have 2 loops on your hook when you pull through.*) CH 1 and turn. Don't cut the White yarn.

Tip: The chain 2 does not count as a stitch, so you want to insert your hook directly into the first stitch from the row below. This saves you from having to insert your hook into the turning chain at the end of the row; instead you can just end on the last stitch.

ROW 3: With Teal, work 1 SC in each stitch across the row. CH 1 and turn.

ROW 4: SC in each stitch across the row. On the last stitch of the row, pull through with White, picking up the strand you left behind and laying it against the side of your work as you pull it up. (*You'll cover this later with the border.*) CH 2 and turn. Leave the Teal yarn uncut so you can come back and pick it up later.

REPEAT ROWS 1 THROUGH 4 for the remainder of the blanket. Work 3 stripes of Pale Teal, 3 stripes of Medium Teal, then 3 stripes of Teal Heather (all with White stripes in between) and then repeat the pattern again starting with Pale Teal. Repeat the pattern 3 more times until you end with Medium Teal.

BORDER

Weave in any ends with a tapestry needle.

ROUND 1: With White, pull up a loop in any corner and CH 3. DC around the entire blanket, working 3 DCs into each corner stitch. *(I found that the border came out the most even on the sides when I worked 2 DCs for the White stripes and only 1 DC for the Teal stripes.)*

ROUND 2: When you reach the corner you started with, work 3 DCs into the corner, then go around the blanket again in the same direction, this time alternating front and back post double crochet (FPDC & BPDC). When you get to the corners of this row, you will want to continue the pattern of alternating FPDC and BPDC, but you will work 3 stitches around the corner post.

So, for example, if you get to the corner post and you are supposed to work a FPDC, then work a FPDC, a BPDC, and a FPDC all around that corner post. Then in the next stitch you would continue the alternating pattern, working the opposite of whichever stitch you just used. Just remember that you are always alternating FPDC and BPDC around the whole blanket, you just happen to be working three of those stitches around the same post when you are working the corners.

ROUND 3: When you finish round 2, work 3 alternating FPDC/BPDC into the corner you started with and repeat round 2 around the blanket. Always match your post double crochets so that they are popping out in the same direction as the previous row.

ROUND 4: To finish off the border, work one row of SC around the blanket, working 3 SCs into each of the corners. When you reach the corner you started with, slip stitch into the starting stitch and fasten off.

CANDY DOTS BABY BLANKET

By Hannah

MATERIALS

YARN Bernat Baby Velvet
(100% polyester, 300 g/10.5 oz, 450 m/492 yds)
4 skeins Misty Gray
1 skein Ever After Pink
1 skein Seafoam
1 skein Joyful Gold
1 skein Cuddly Cloud

HOOK Size H, 5.00mm hook

TOOLS Tapestry needle, Scissors

SIZE Finished size: 36 in x 36 in
Gauge: 4 in = 16 stitches and 12 rows

STITCHES

WIDE HALF DOUBLE CROCHET (WHDC): Yarn over (YO), insert your hook in between the posts of the row below (under all 3 loops of stitch), YO and pull up a loop, YO, pull through all 3 loops on hook.

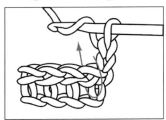

PUFF STITCH: *YO, insert your hook into designated space, YO and pull up a loop. Repeat from * 3 more times (inserting your hook into the same space). Then YO and pull through all the loops on your hook.

DOUBLE CROCHET (DC): YO, insert your hook, YO and pull up a loop, YO, pull through two loops, YO, pull through remaining two loops on your hook.

FRONT & BACK POST DOUBLE CROCHET (FPDC & BPDC): A front post double crochet means you insert your hook from front to back around the post of the next DC and work a DC. A back post double crochet means you insert your hook from back to front around the post of the next DC and work a DC.

PATTERN

CHAIN 121 with Gray. (Pattern repeat is any multiple of 5, plus 1.)

ROW 1: Starting in the 3rd chain from the hook, work 1 HDC. Work 1 HDC in each chain across the row. CH 2 and turn.

ROWS 2 - 5: Work 1 WHDC in each space across the row. CH 2 and turn.
(From now on you will always be inserting your hook in between the posts of the previous row, even on the puff stitches.)

ROW 6: Work 1 WHDC in each of the first 4 spaces with Gray. On the 4th stitch, pull through with Pink. Work 1 puff stitch with Pink, carrying the Gray along your work and crocheting over it. Right before you finish the puff stitch, pull through with Gray. *Work 1 WHDC in the next 4 spaces with Gray, carrying the Pink yarn along your work and crocheting over it as you go. On the next stitch, work 1 puff stitch with Pink, carrying the Gray along your work and crocheting over it. Right before you finish the puff stitch, pull through with Gray. Repeat from * to the end of the row. CH 2 and turn. Cut the Pink, leaving a tail long enough to weave into the blanket later.

Tip: As I was working this row I found the best way to keep my yarn from twisting as I carried it across the row was to make sure that I always kept the Gray to the front and the Pink to the back of my work each time I switched colors.

ROW 7: With Gray, work 1 WHDC in each space across the row, inserting your hook in the spaces between the stitches and also underneath the yarn that you carried through on the row below. *(Sometimes it can be a little tricky to see, but this helps to make sure that the carried yarn doesn't show through on either side.)* When you get to the puffs, make sure and work 1 stitch on either side of them. CH 2 and turn.

ROWS 8 - 11: Work 1 WHDC in each space across the row with Gray. CH 2 and turn. (4 rows of Gray.)

REPEAT ROWS 6 TO 11 for the remainder of the blanket, changing colors each time you repeat row 6. In other words, you are working *5 rows Gray, 1 row with Pink puffs, 5 rows Gray, 1 row with Seafoam puffs, 5 rows Gray, 1 row with Gold puffs, 5 rows Gray, 1 row with White puffs, 5 rows Gray. Repeat from * until you reach your desired length.

I decided to end with 1 row of Pink puffs before my last 5 rows of Gray to match the first Pink puff row on the other end of the blanket. So in total, I had 21 puff rows when I was finished.

BORDER

Weave in all ends with a tapestry needle.

ROUND 1: With Misty Gray, pull up a loop in any corner and CH 3. DC around the entire blanket, working 3 DCs into each corner stitch.

ROUND 2: When you reach the corner you started with, work 3 DCs into the corner, then go around the blanket again in the same direction, this time alternating front and back post double crochet (FPDC & BPDC). When you get to the corners of this row, you will want to continue the pattern of alternating FPDC and BPDC, but you will work 3 stitches around the corner post.

So, for example, if you get to the corner post and you are supposed to work a FPDC, then work a FPDC, a BPDC, and a FPDC all around that corner post. Then in the next stitch you would continue the alternating pattern, working the opposite of whichever stitch you just used. Just remember that you are always alternating FPDC and BPDC around the whole blanket, you just happen to be working three of those stitches around the same post when you are working the corners.

ROUND 3: When you finish round 2, work 3 alternating FPDC/BPDC into the corner you started with and repeat round 2 around the blanket. Always match your post double crochets so that they are poking out in the same direction as the previous row.

ROUND 4: Repeat round 3. When you reach the corner you stared with, slip stitch into the corner and tie off.

NOTES

For this blanket I used Bernat Baby Velvet yarn which is so soft and luscious but is not without its challenges. Here are a few rules we've made for ourselves after using this yarn:

DON'T PULL FROM THE MIDDLE. For whatever reason, every time we've tried pulling yarn from the middle of the skein while we are crocheting, it always ends up getting tangled. Things go much better when we unwind the yarn from the outside of the skein. My younger sisters have even gone so far as to roll the whole skein into a ball before they start crocheting.

KEEP YOUR TENSION TIGHT. I tend to be a loose crocheter in general, so I have to really pay attention with this yarn to make sure my tension stays tight the whole time to avoid any loose loops coming up. When it comes to velvet, the tighter the stitches the better. Work a practice swatch to make sure you have the correct tension.

WASH DELICATELY. Baby Velvet is machine washable, but washing it on a delicate setting will help avoid any loose stitches in the blanket from pulling up.

Please also note that the colors I used for the dots in this blanket were only available in the bigger 10.5oz skeins, but if you find a different color you'd like to use for one of the dot colors that is available in the 3.5oz size skein, that size is also enough for the dots.

If you'd like to add finishing touches to your blanket, lay it out flat on a towel or foam blocking boards if you have them. Use a spray bottle with water to dampen the blanket. Press the blanket into straight lines, massaging the stitches and adjusting your tension. Pin with straight pins to let it dry.

COUNTRY BLUE STRIPES BABY BLANKET

By Tiffany

MATERIALS

YARN   Caron Simply Soft
(100% acrylic, 170 g/6 oz, 288 m/315 yds)
2 skeins White
1 skein Light Country Blue
1 skein Country Blue
1 skein Pumpkin

HOOK   Size H, 5.00mm hook

TOOLS   Tapestry needle, Scissors

SIZE   Finished size: 34 in x 36 in
Gauge: 4 in = 14 stitches and 14 rows

STITCHES

HALF DOUBLE CROCHET TWO TOGETHER (HDC2TOG) CLUSTER: Yarn over (YO) and insert your hook into the indicated stitch, YO and pull a loop back through. YO and insert your hook into the next stitch, YO and pull a loop back through. YO and pull through all 5 loops on your hook.

DOUBLE CROCHET (DC): YO, insert your hook, YO and pull up a loop, YO and pull through first two loops on hook, YO and pull through remaining two loops on hook.

HERRINGBONE HALF DOUBLE CROCHET (HHDC): YO, insert your hook, YO and pull up a loop and pull directly through first loop on hook. Then YO and pull through remaining loops on hook.

PATTERN

CHAIN 115 with White. (Pattern repeat is any odd number.)

2 rows White
2 rows Pumpkin
2 rows White
2 rows Dark Country Blue
4 rows White
3 rows Light Country Blue
6 rows Dark Country Blue
2 rows White
2 rows Light Country Blue
2 rows White
2 rows Pumpkin
2 rows White
3 rows Dark Country Blue
6 rows Light Country Blue
2 rows White
2 rows Dark Country Blue
2 rows White
2 rows Pumpkin
2 rows White
3 rows Light Country Blue
6 rows Dark Country Blue
4 rows White
2 rows Light Country Blue
2 rows White
2 rows Pumpkin
2 rows White

ROW 1: With White, work 1 HDC2tog cluster across the 4th and 5th chain from the hook. (YO, insert hook in 4th chain from the hook, YO and pull a loop back through, YO, insert hook in 5th chain from hook, YO and pull a loop back through, YO and pull through all loops on hook.) In 5th chain, work 1 DC.

*Work 1 HDC2tog cluster across next 2 stitches, 1 DC in the second stitch (meaning the stitch where the last leg of the HDC2tog cluster landed.) Repeat from * across the row.

Work 1 HDC2tog cluster across the last stitch of the row and the top of the skipped 3 starting chains. CH 3 and turn.

ROW 2: Work 1 HDC2tog cluster across the first 2 stitches of the row, 1 DC in the second stitch. *Work 1 HDC2tog cluster across next 2 stitches, 1 DC in the second stitch. Repeat from * across the row. Work 1 HDC2tog across the last stitch and the top of the turning chain. CH 3 and turn.

ROW 3 TO END OF BLANKET: Repeat row 2.

COLOR CHANGES:

2 rows White, 2 rows Pumpkin, 2 rows White, 2 rows Light Country Blue, 4 rows White, 6 rows Dark Country Blue, 3 rows Light Country Blue, 2 rows White, 2 rows Pumpkin, 2 rows White, 2 rows Dark Country Blue, 2 rows White, 6 rows Light Country Blue, 3 rows Dark Country Blue, 2 rows White, 2 rows Pumpkin, 2 rows White, 2 rows Light Country Blue, 2 rows White, 6 rows Dark Country Blue, 3 rows Light Country Blue, 4 rows White, 2 rows Dark Country Blue, 2 rows White, 2 rows Pumpkin, 2 rows White.

BORDER

Weave in all ends with a tapestry needle.

ROUND 1: With White, pull up a loop in any corner, CH 1 and SC in that space. Work 1 SC into each stitch across the top and bottom of the blanket, work 3 SC into each corner and work approximately 3 SC per 2 rows along the sides of the blanket. (Work your SC as evenly as possible on the sides of the blanket.) Slip stitch to starting SC.

ROUNDS 2 AND 3: Continue in the same direction and work 1 HHDC into each stitch. Work 3 HHDC into each corner stitch. At the end of the 3rd round, join with a slip stitch, chain 2 and turn.

ROUNDS 4 AND 5: Work the HHDC in each stitch. Work 3 HHDC into each corner stitch. At the end of the 5th round continue with one round of all SC.

ROUND 6: Work SC into each stitch, work 3 SC into each corner. Tie off and weave in all ends when finished with the round.

TRIANGLES BABY BLANKET

By Hannah

MATERIALS

YARN Bernat Softee Baby
(100% acrylic, 140g /5 oz, 331 m/362 yds)
5 skeins Soft Peach
1 skein White

HOOK Size H, 5.00mm hook

TOOLS Tapestry needle, Scissors

SIZE Finished size: 31 in x 31 in
Gauge: 4 in = 16 stitches and 12 rows

STITCHES

WIDE HALF DOUBLE CROCHET (WHDC) CLUSTER: Yarn over (YO), insert hook in between the posts of the row below, YO and pull up a loop, YO, insert hook again into same space, YO and pull up another loop, YO, pull through all loops on hook.

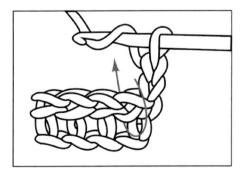

DOUBLE CROCHET (DC): YO, insert your hook, YO and pull up a loop, YO, pull through two loops, YO, pull through remaining two loops on your hook.

FRONT AND BACK POST DOUBLE CROCHET (FPDC & BPDC): A front post double crochet means you insert your hook from front to back around the post of the next DC and work a DC. A back post double crochet means you insert your hook from back to front around the post of the next DC and work a DC.

Changing colors: Pull through with the new color just before you finish the WHDC cluster stitch, when you have five loops on your hook. To avoid your yarn getting twisted as you carry it along your work, it helps to always keep one color to the front and one color to the back. So whenever I would switch from Peach to White, I would keep the Peach to the back and crochet over it, but when switching from White back to Peach, I would wrap the White to the front of my work before starting to crochet over it.

PATTERN

CHAIN 87 with Soft Peach. *(Pattern repeat is a multiple of 10, plus 7. If you are using the same yarn as I did, the base chain may seem too short at first, but it will stretch out after a few rows.)*

ROW 1: Starting in the 3rd chain from the hook, work 1 WHDC cluster in each chain. CH 2 and turn.

ROWS 2 - 5: Work 1 WHDC cluster into each space between the stitches across the row. *(Make sure you don't miss the last space at the end of the row between the last stitch and the turning chain.)* CH 2 and turn.

ROW 6: Work 1 WHDC cluster in each of the first 5 spaces with Soft Peach. On the 5th stitch, stop just before you finish the stitch when you still have five loops on your hook, and pull through with White. Leave a 6 inch tail with White that you can weave into the blanket later. *Now work 1 WHDC cluster in each of the next 5 spaces with White, carrying the Soft Peach along the top of your work and crocheting over it as you go. On the 5th stitch, pull through with Soft Peach before you finish the stitch. Work a WHDC cluster in each of the next 5 spaces with Soft Peach, carrying the White along the top of your work. Repeat from * to the end of the row until you end with 5 WHDC clusters in Soft Peach. CH 2 and turn.

ROW 7: Wrap the White around the back of your work and crochet over it as you work a WHDC cluster in each of the next 5 spaces with Soft Peach. On the 5th stitch, pull through with White. *WHDC cluster in each of the next 4 spaces with White, then WHDC cluster in each of the next 6 spaces with Soft Peach. Repeat from * to the end of the row, until you end with 6 WHDC clusters in Soft Peach. CH 2 and turn.

ROW 8: Wrap the White around the back of your work and crochet over it as you work a WHDC cluster in each of the next 6 stitches with Soft Peach. On the 6th stitch, pull through with White. *WHDC cluster in each of the next 3 spaces with White, then WHDC cluster in each of the next 7 spaces with Soft Peach. Repeat from * to the end of the row, until you end with 6 WHDC clusters in Soft Peach. CH 2 and turn.

ROW 9: Wrap the White around the back of your work and crochet over it as you work work a WHDC cluster in each of the next 6 spaces with Soft Peach. On the 6th stitch, pull through with White. *WHDC cluster in each of the next 2 spaces with White, then WHDC cluster in each of the next 8 spaces with Soft Peach. Repeat from * to the end of the row, until you end with 7 WHDC clusters in Soft Peach. CH 2 and turn.

ROW 10: Wrap the White around the back of your work and crochet over it as you work work a WHDC cluster in each of the next 7 spaces with Soft Peach. On the 7th stitch, pull through with White. *WHDC cluster in the next space with White, then WHDC cluster in each of the next 9 spaces with Soft Peach. Repeat from * to the end of the row, until you end with 7 WHDC clusters in Soft Peach. CH 2 and turn.

ROWS 11 - 15: Cut the White yarn and leave a tail long enough to weave into the blanket later. Work 1 WHDC cluster in each space across the row with Soft Peach. CH 2 and turn.

ROW 16: Work a WHDC cluster in each of the next 10 spaces with Soft Peach. On the 10th stitch, pull through with White. *WHDC cluster in each of the next 5 spaces with White, then WHDC in the each of the next 5 spaces with Soft Peach. Repeat from * to the end of the row, and end the row with 10 WHDC clusters in Soft Peach. CH 2 and turn.

ROW 17: Wrap the White around the back of your work and crochet over it as you work work a WHDC cluster in each of the next 10 spaces with Soft Peach. On the 10th stitch, pull through with White. *WHDC cluster in each of the next 4 spaces with White, then WHDC cluster in each of the next 6 spaces with Soft Peach. Repeat from * to the end of the row, until you end with 11 WHDC clusters in Soft Peach. CH 2 and turn.

ROW 18: Wrap the White around the back of your work and crochet over it as you work a WHDC cluster in each of the next 11 spaces with Soft Peach. On the 11th stitch, pull through with White. *WHDC cluster in each of the next 3 spaces with White, then WHDC cluster in each of the next 7 spaces with Soft Peach. Repeat from * to the end of the row, until you end with 11 WHDC clusters in Soft Peach. CH 2 and turn.

ROW 19: Wrap the White around the back of your work and crochet over it as you work a WHDC cluster in each of the next 11 spaces with Soft Peach. On the 11th stitch, pull through with White. *WHDC cluster in each of the next 2 spaces with White, then WHDC cluster in each of the next 8 spaces with Soft Peach. Repeat from * to the end of the row, until you end with 12 wide HDC clusters in Soft Peach. CH 2 and turn.

ROW 20: Wrap the White around the back of your work and crochet over it as you work a WHDC cluster in each of the next 12 spaces with Soft Peach. On the 12th stitch, pull through with White. *WHDC cluster in the next space with White, then WHDC cluster in each of the next 9 spaces with Soft Peach. Repeat from * to the end of the row, until you end with 12 WHDC clusters in Soft Peach. CH 2 and turn.

ROWS 21 - 25: Cut the White yarn and leave a tail long enough to weave into the blanket later. Work a WHDC cluster in each space across the row with Soft Peach. CH 2 and turn.

REPEAT ROWS 6 THROUGH 25 for the remainder of the blanket. I ended up with 9 sets of triangles when my blanket was the length I wanted.

Even though I wrote out the counts for each row in this pattern, as I was making this blanket, I really only focused on the counting for the bottom rows of my triangles so that they were evenly spaced and lined up; after that I just visually built my triangles by decreasing the white stitches by one on each row.

BORDER

Weave in all ends with a tapestry needle.

ROUND 1: With Soft Peach, pull up a loop in any corner and CH 3. Work one round of DC around the blanket, working one DC per row on the sides and still working in between the posts on the ends of the blanket. Work 5 DCs into each corner.

ROUND 2: When you reach the corner you started with, work 5 DCs into the corner, then go around the blanket again in the same direction, this time alternating front and back post double crochet (FPDC & BPDC). When you get to the corners of this row, you will want to continue the pattern of alternating FPDC and BPDC, but you will work 3 stitches around the corner post.

So, for example, if you get to the corner post and you are supposed to work a FPDC, then work a FPDC, a BPDC, and a FPDC all around that corner post. Then in the next stitch you would continue the alternating pattern, working the opposite of whichever stitch you just used. Just remember that you are always alternating FPDC and BPDC around the whole blanket, you just happen to be working three of those stitches around the same post when you are working the corners.

ROUND 3: When you finish round 2, work 3 alternating FPDC/BPDC into the corner you started with and repeat round 2 around the blanket. Always match your post double crochets so that they are poking out in the same direction as the previous row.

ROUND 4: Repeat round 3. When you are finished with your border, slip stitch into the starting stitch and tie off.

If you'd like to add finishing touches to your blanket, lay it out flat on a towel or foam blocking boards if you have them. Use a spray bottle with water to dampen the blanket. Press the blanket into straight lines, massaging the stitches and adjusting your tension. Pin with straight pins and let it dry.

NAUTICAL BABY BLANKET

By Tiffany

MATERIALS

YARN Bernat Softee Baby
(100% acrylic, 140g/5 oz, 331 m/362 yds)
2 skeins White
1 skein Aqua
1 skein Royal Blue

HOOK Size G, 4.00mm hook

TOOLS Tapestry needle, Scissors

SIZE Finished size: 34 in x 34 in
Gauge: 4 in = 22 stitches and 18 rows

STITCHES

SINGLE CROCHET (SC): Insert your hook, yarn over (YO) and pull up a loop, YO and pull through both loops on your hook.

HALF DOUBLE CROCHET (HDC): YO, insert your hook, YO and pull up a loop, YO, pull through three loops.

DOUBLE CROCHET (DC): YO, insert your hook, YO and pull up a loop, YO, pull through two loops, YO, pull through remaining two loops on your hook.

PATTERN

CHAIN 141 with Royal Blue. (The pattern repeat is any multiple of 3.)

ROW 1: In the 2nd chain from the hook, work "SC, CH, DC", *skip 2 chains, work "SC, CH, DC" in the next chain. Repeat from * to the end of the row and until you have 1 remaining chain space. Work 1 SC in the last remaining chain space. CH 1 and turn.

ROW 2: "SC, CH, DC" in the top of the first SC of the row below. *Skip the next two stitches. Work "SC, CH, DC" into the SC stitch of the row below. Repeat from * ending the row with 1 SC in the very last stitch, CH 1 and turn.

ROW 3: Repeat Row 2.

REPEAT ROW 3 for the rest of the blanket, changing colors every 10th row.

COLOR CHANGES: 10 rows Royal Blue, 10 rows White, 10 Rows Aqua, 10 Rows White. Repeat 2 times, then work 10 Blue, 10 White, 10 Aqua. (I ended on an Aqua stripe.)

Weave in all ends before you start the border.

BORDER

With White, pull up a loop in any corner. SC around the entire blanket working 3 SC in each corner and keeping them as evenly spaced as possible. If they are too close, your border will ruffle, too far apart and the main blanket will pucker. This is where you as the crochet artist will decide where each stitch will go. For me, it worked to skip every third stitch on the top and bottom of the blanket, and to work 10 SC per color on the sides of the blanket. It's more important to crochet evenly than worry about numbers.

Slip stitch to the starting SC. Continuing on in the same direction, CH 10. In the 3rd chain from the hook, work 1 HDC. Work 1 HDC in each of the remaining 7 chains. SL ST into the next SC on the edge of the blanket, and SL ST into the next SC (2 SL ST). *Turn the border, like a page in a book, and work 1 Back Loop Only HDC in each of the 8 HDC. CH 1 and turn. Work 1 Back Loop Only HDC in each of the 8 HDC back toward the edge of the blanket. SL ST into the next 2 spaces. Repeat from * down the side of the blanket.

When you approach the 3 SC that make the corner, only SL ST once in the first SC, work the back loop HDC's up and back down, then SL ST once to the corner SC, work the Back Loop Only HDC up and back down again, and SL ST into the SAME corner stitch again, and then again for a total of 3 times. This will fan the work around the corner. Then SL ST once into the third SC of the corner SC's, work the Back Loop Only HDC's up and back down, then continue on down the next side slip stitching every 2 spaces again as before.

Tip: Check your work as you go; I would undo and redo if the border was looking rippled and slip stitch into 3 stitches if needed.

Upon returning to the starting HDC's, end after you work the Back Loop Only HDC up, then fasten off, use your tapestry needle to sew the two sides together, then weave in the ends.

FRONT LOOP CHEVRON BABY BLANKET

By Tiffany

MATERIALS

YARN   Caron Simply Soft
(100% acrylic, 170 g/6 oz, 288 m/315 yds)
3 skeins Gold
1 skein White

HOOK   Size I, 5.50mm hook

TOOLS   Tapestry needle, Scissors

SIZE   Finished size: 32 in x 34 in
Gauge: 2 in = 9 stitches and 8 rows

STITCHES

SINGLE CROCHET (SC): Insert your hook, yarn over (YO) and pull up a loop, YO and pull through both loops on your hook.

SINGLE CROCHET TWO TOGETHER (SC2TOG): Insert your hook into the first chain, YO and pull up a loop, insert your hook into the next chain, YO and pull up a loop, yarn over and pull through all loops on your hook.

PATTERN

CHAIN 177 with Gold. (Pattern repeat is any multiple of 29, plus 3.)

ROW 1: In the 2nd chain from the hook and the next chain, SC2TOG (insert your hook into the first chain, pull up a loop, insert your hook into the next chain, pull up a loop, yarn over and pull through all loops on your hook). *SC in the next 13 chains, work 3 SC into the next chain, SC in the next 13 chains, skip 2 chains. Repeat from *. After you have worked the last 13 chains, you should have two extra. SC2TOG these last two stitches. CH 1 and turn.

ROW 2: Now, start the next row by SC2TOG, inserting your hook into the front loop of each stitch. (From now on you will always be working only into the front loop.) *SC in the next 13 stitches, then 3 SC into the next stitch (this should be the middle stitch of the 3 SC you did in the row before), SC in the next 13 stitches, skip 2 stitches at the bottom for the valley, and repeat from *. After you have worked the last 13 chains, you should have two extra. SC2TOG these last two stitches. CH 1 and turn.

REPEAT ROW 2 for the remainder of the blanket. Always remember to SC2TOG each time you start and end a row. Always skip two stitches for a valley, always work 13 up each side. Always work 3 SC into one stitch for the peak. Always CH 1 and turn.

COLOR CHANGES: Start with 9 rows of Gold, then alternate 1 row White and 1 row Gold a total of five times. Work 9 rows of Gold in between the alternating White and Gold rows. When you reach your desired length, end with 9 rows of Gold. I had 5 sections of alternating color for the size I made.

When you are changing colors, you want to pull through with the new color just before you finish the SC2TOG at the end of the row (you should have 3 loops on your hook when you pull through.) Then you'll cut the yarn of the first color, leaving a tail long enough to weave in later. When you finish your blanket, tie off and weave in all your ends with a tapestry needle.

BORDER

For the border, I worked 1 round of SC in Gold around the outside of the blanket.

To do this, pull up a loop in any corner and CH 1. SC in each stitch on the sides, and on the ends work 3 SCs into the peaks and skip the two stitches of the valleys, just as you did when working the regular pattern. Work 3 SCs into each of the corners of the blanket.

When you reach the corner you started with, slip stitch into the corner and tie off and weave that end in.

After I finished my blanket I laid it out flat and used a spray bottle to get it wet with water and smoothed out all the sides to block it before letting it dry overnight. It's normal to have the sides of the blanket curl in on you, but blocking the blanket will smooth everything out.

CACTUS BABY BLANKET

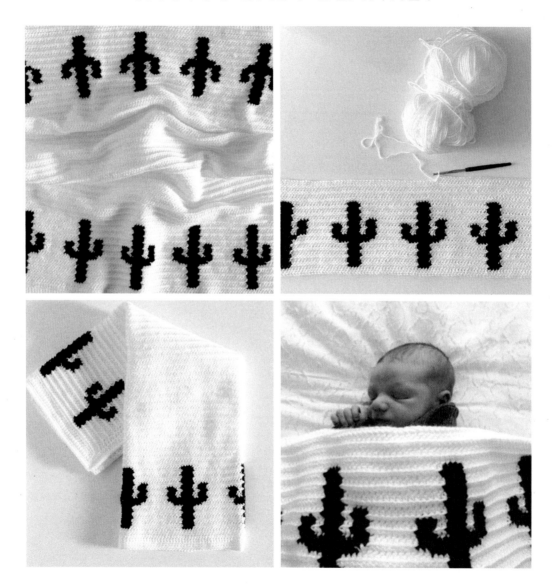

By Tiffany

MATERIALS

YARN   Red Heart Soft
(100% acrylic, 283 g/10 oz, 469 m/513 yds)
3 skeins White
1 skein Black

HOOK   Size H, 5.00mm hook

TOOLS   Tapestry needle, Scissors, Ziploc plastic bags

SIZE   Finished size: 32 in x 34 in
Gauge: 4 in = 16 stitches and 14 rows

STITCHES

SINGLE CROCHET (SC): Insert your hook, yarn over (YO) and pull up a loop, YO and pull through both loops on your hook.

HALF DOUBLE CROCHET (HDC): YO, insert your hook, YO and pull up a loop, YO, pull through three loops.

FRONT 2 LOOP HALF DOUBLE CROCHET (F2LPHDC): YO and work your hook up and under the front two loops (the two loops that face you) of the half double crochet stitch, YO and pull up a loop, YO and pull through all three loops on the hook, stitch complete.

PATTERN

Tip: Before starting, wind fist size balls of black yarn and place each one into the Ziploc bags - one per bag and one bag per each cactus. Try using the slide close type Ziploc bag for best results.

CHAIN 114 with White. (Pattern repeat is 22, plus 4. Multiply the number of cactus you would like across the end of your blanket times 22, then add 4.)

ROW 1: In the 3rd chain from the hook, work 1 HDC. Work 1 HDC in each chain across the row. CH 2 and turn. (112)

ROW 2: In first stitch, (turning chain does not count as a stitch) work 1 F2LPHDC. Work 1 F2LPHDC in each stitch across the row. CH 2 and turn. (112)

ROWS 3 - 21: Using the F2LPHDC now and throughout the entire blanket, start in the lower right hand corner of the chart and follow the graph. To change color, pull through on the last step of the stitch. Use one ball of Black yarn per cactus. You will carry the White yarn through the Black (this means the White yarn will lie flat across the row and you will crochet over it and bring it through the Black portion of the cactus.)

ROWS 22 - 66: Repeat row 2.

ROW 67-85: Turn the graph upside down and work the cactus from the top to the bottom.

ROWS 86 - 87: Repeat row 2. Tie off and weave in the ends.

BORDER

ROUND 1: With White, pull up a loop in any corner and CH 1. Work 1 HDC in each stitch across the row, and work 1 HDC and the end of each row on the sides of the blanket. Work 3 HDC into each corner. Join with a slip stitch to the starting HDC.

ROUNDS 2 AND 3: Continuing in the same direction, work 1 SC into each stitch. Work 3 SC into each corner. Join with a slip stitch at the end of round 3. Tie off and weave in all ends.

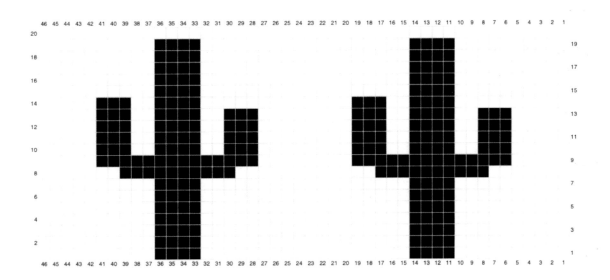

SEDGE STRIPES BABY BLANKET

By Nicolina

MATERIALS

YARN   Red Heart Soft Essentials
(100% acrylic, 141 g/5 oz, 120 m/131 yds)
2 skeins White
3 skeins Greyhound
1 skein Peony

HOOK   Size J, 6.00mm hook

TOOLS   Tapestry needle, Scissors

SIZE   Finished size: 30 in x 32 in
Gauge: 4 in = 12 stitches and 9 rows

STITCHES

SINGLE CROCHET (SC): Insert your hook, yarn over (YO) and pull up a loop, YO, pull through two loops.

HALF DOUBLE CROCHET (HDC): YO, insert your hook, YO and pull up a loop, YO, pull through three loops.

DOUBLE CROCHET (DC): YO, insert your hook, YO and pull up a loop, YO, pull through two loops, YO, pull through last two loops.

PATTERN

CHAIN 99 with Greyhound. (Pattern repeat is any multiple of 3.)

ROW 1: In the second chain from the hook, work 1 HDC and 1 DC, skip two chains and in the next chain work "SC, HDC, DC." Skip two chains and repeat "SC, HDC, DC" into the next space. Repeat across to the end until there is one chain left. Work 1 SC in that chain and turn.

ROW 2: CH one (this counts as your first SC), work 1 HDC and 1 DC into the top of the SC you just made in the row below. Skip over the next 2 stitches, "SC, HDC, DC" into the SC. (You'll always be looking for the SC to work your "SC, HDC, DC" into.) Repeat the pattern across ending the last stitch with one SC. CH one and turn.

REPEAT ROW 2 FOR THE REMAINDER OF THE BLANKET.

COLOR CHANGES: 8 rows Greyhound, 4 rows White, 2 rows Peony, 2 rows White, 4 rows Greyhound, 2 rows White, 4 rows Peony, 4 rows White, 4 rows Greyhound, 2 rows White, 2 rows Peony, 4 rows White, 4 rows Greyhound, 4 rows White, 4 rows Peony, 2 rows White, 4 rows Greyhound, 2 rows White, 2 rows Peony, 4 rows White, 8 rows Greyhound.

When changing colors, you want to pull through with the new color on the last SC of the row. Pull through with the new color just before you finish the stitch, when you still have two loops on your hook.

Then cut off the old color, leaving about a six inch tail that you can weave into the blanket with a tapestry needle later. When you are finished with the blanket, tie off and weave in ends. I decided to not do a border. The sides of the blanket have a nice texture and I didn't think a border was necessary.

TEXTURED LINES BABY BLANKET

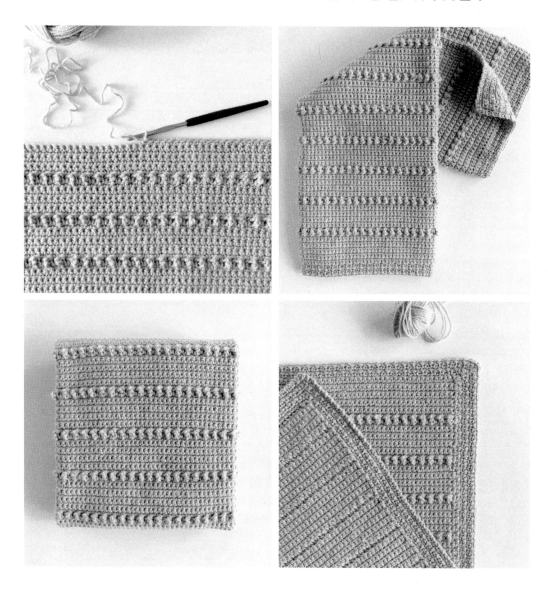

By Annie

MATERIALS

YARN   Paton's Canadiana
(100% acrylic, 100 g/3.5 oz, 187 m/205 yds)
5 skeins Pale Blue

HOOK   Size H, 5.00mm hook

TOOLS   Tapestry needle, Scissors

SIZE   Finished size: 26 in x 26 in
Gauge: 4 in = 17 stitches and 20 rows

STITCHES

SINGLE CROCHET (SC): Insert your hook, yarn over (YO) and pull up a loop, YO and pull through both loops on your hook.

TREBLE CROCHET (TC): YO twice, insert your hook into the designated stitch, YO and pull up a loop, YO and pull through two loops, YO and pull through two loops again, YO and pull through remaining two loops left on the hook.

PATTERN

CHAIN 100 (or any even number).

ROW 1: In the 2nd chain from the hook, work 1 SC. SC into each chain across the row. (99 SC made.) CH 1 and turn.

ROWS 2 - 7: Work 1 SC into each stitch from the row below. CH 1 and turn.

ROW 8: *Work 1 SC into the first SC from the row below, work 1 TC into the next SC from the row below. Repeat from * across the row. CH 1 and turn.

Tip: Your first and last stitch of row 8, (the textured row) will be a single crochet.

REPEAT ROWS 1 THROUGH 8 until you have 11 textured rows. (You should have 7 rows of SC between each textured row.) Finish last 7 rows with instructions from row 1 - 7. Tie off and weave in ends before you start the border.

BORDER

ROUND 1: In any corner and with the textured side facing you, pull up a loop and SC in that space. *CH 1, skip the next stitch, SC into the next. Repeat from * around the sides and ends of blanket. When arriving at the corners, work 3 SC. Join the round by finishing the starting corner with 2 SC and join with a slip stitch to the first SC made. CH 1 and turn.

Tip: The second round will have you work SC into the tops of SC and CH across the CH from the row below. This is called the Mesh Stitch. The stitches stack on top of each other.

ROUNDS 2 - 5: Work 3 SC into the corner stitch from the row below.

Then, look ahead a few stitches and figure out if you need to start the round with a CH or a SC.

You want your stitches to stack on top of each other to make the mesh stitch. You will still always work 3 SC into the middle SC that makes the corner.

Also, as the rounds grow around the corners, sometimes you will be working a CH across a SC in order to keep the mesh stitch consistent.

Join each round with a slip stitch, CH 1 and turn.

Tie off and weave in the ends.

MESH HALF STRIPES BABY BLANKET

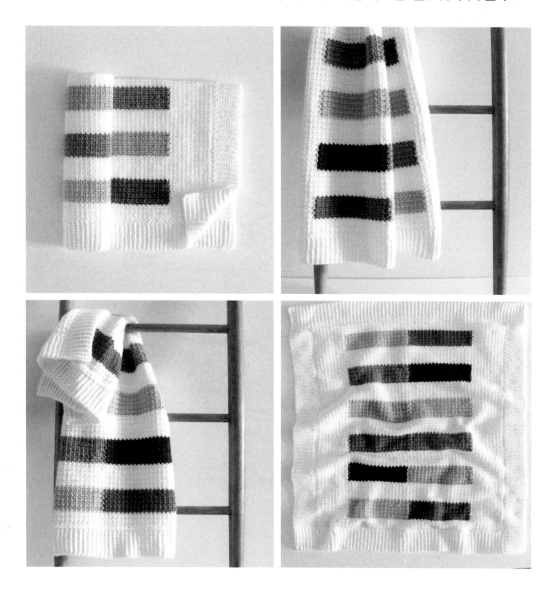

By Tiffany

MATERIALS

YARN   Caron Simply Soft
(100% acrylic, 170 g/6 oz, 288 m 315 yds)
4 skeins White
1 skein each of Light Country Blue, Country Blue, Dark Country Blue, Gold
and Gray Heather

HOOK   Size H, 5.00mm hook

TOOLS   Tapestry needle, Scissors

SIZE   Finished size: 28 in x 31 in
Gauge: 4 in = 20 stitches and 20 rows

STITCHES

SINGLE CROCHET (SC): Insert your hook, yarn over (YO) and pull up a loop, YO and pull through both loops on your hook.

SLIP STITCH (SL ST): Insert your hook, YO and pull up a loop and pull directly through loops on hook.

HALF DOUBLE CROCHET (HDC): YO, insert your hook, YO and pull up a loop, YO and pull through all three loops.

HALF DOUBLE CROCHET SLIP STITCH (HDSS): YO, insert your hook, YO and pull up a loop and pull directly through all loops on hook.

PATTERN

COLOR SEQUENCE: *Color A: Country Blue, Color B: Gold, Color C: Light Country Blue, Color D: Dark Country Blue, Color E: Gray Heather*

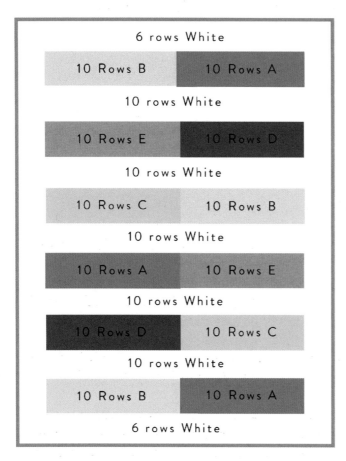

CHAIN 110 with White.

ROW 1: Begin in the 2nd chain from the hook. *SC, CH 1, skip the next CH and SC into the next. Repeat from * across the row. CH 1 and turn.

ROWS 2 - 6: *SC into SC from the row below, CH 1, skip the next CH, SC into the next SC. Repeat from * across the row, CH 1 and turn.

(This repeated sequence is called the Mesh Stitch and will be repeated throughout the rest of the blanket. What follows is the color changing instructions.)

ROW 7: Work the Mesh Stitch until the 10th SC. In the 10th SC, pull through with Color A, CH 1 with new color, work Mesh Stitch across the next 18 SC, leaving the White behind to be picked up on the return pass.

In the 18th SC, pull through with Color B, CH 1 with new color, leave Color A behind, and work the Mesh Stitch across the next 18 SC. In the 18th SC, pull through with White (use a new skein). Work the Mesh Stitch to the end of the row, (there will be 9 SC's) CH 1 and turn.

For the rest of the blanket continue with the Mesh Stitch and working the color changes and row counts according to the graph.

BORDER

ROUND 1: After completing the last row of the blanket, don't turn. Work 2 more SC into the last stitch. CH 1 and begin working the Mesh Stitch around 3 sides of the blanket, working one SC into the side of one row, and 1 CH across the side of the next row. End with 1 SC in the 4th corner.

SIDE 1: Do not turn, CH 12. In the 3rd chain from the hook, work 1 HDC.

Tip: for the best looking result, work under both loops of the chain, not just the top loop.

HDC into each of the chain spaces. SL ST to the next stitch on the blanket. *Turn and work HDSS into each of the next 10 HDC. CH 1 and turn. HDSS into each stitch (10), SL ST into the next 2 stitches on the blanket. Repeat from * working down the side.

Tip: If your border is ruffling, add more slip stitches in between each row of HDSS. If the opposite is happening and the blanket is rippling, decrease the number of slip stitches.

SIDE 2: Work the first side to the middle stitch of the corner and end your work on the outside edge. CH 12. Rotate the blanket so that you are working up the next side. In the 3rd chain from the hook, work 1 HDC. HDC into each of the next 10 chain spaces. SL ST to the next stitch on the blanket. *Turn and work HDSS into each of the next 10 HDC.

CH 1 and turn. HDSS into each stitch (10) SL ST into the next 2 stitches. Repeat from *
working down the side.

Repeat the instructions for Side 2 for Side 3 and 4. When you've returned to the starting
side, SL ST and cut.

Weave in all the ends with a tapestry needle.

If you'd like to add finishing touches to your blanket, lay it out flat on a towel or foam
blocking boards if you have them. Use a spray bottle with water to dampen the blanket.
Press the blanket into straight lines, massaging the stitches and adjusting your tension. Pin
with straight pins to let it dry.

BERRY CHEVRON BABY BLANKET

By Hannah

MATERIALS

YARN   Bernat Softee Baby
(100% acrylic, 140 g/5 oz, 331 m/362 yds)
3 skeins White
2 skeins Soft Peach

HOOK   Size G, 4.00mm hook

TOOLS   Tapestry needle, Scissors

SIZE   Finished size: 30 in x 38 in
Gauge: 4 in = 16 stitches and 13 rows

STITCHES

SINGLE CROCHET (SC): Insert your hook, yarn over (YO) and pull up a loop, YO and pull through both loops on your hook.

SINGLE CROCHET TWO TOGETHER (SC2TOG): Insert your hook into the first chain, YO and pull up a loop, insert your hook into the next chain, YO and pull up a loop, YO and pull through all loops on your hook.

BERRY STITCH: YO, insert your hook, YO and pull up a loop, YO pull through ONE loop on the hook, YO, insert hook, YO and pull up a loop, YO, pull through all five loops left on hook.

PATTERN

CHAIN 177 with White. (Pattern repeat is a multiple of 29, plus 3.)

ROW 1: SC2TOG across the 2nd and 3rd chain from the hook. *1 SC in each of the next 13 chains, work 3 SC into the next chain, 1 SC in each of the next 13 chains, skip 2 chains. Repeat from * across the row. After you have worked the last 13 chains, you should have two extra. SC2TOG across the last two stitches. CH 1 and turn.

ROWS 2 - 3: SC2TOG across the 1st and 2nd stitches from the hook. *1 SC in each of the next 13 stitches, 3 SC into the next stitch, 1 SC in each of the next 13 stitches, skip 2 stitches. Repeat from * across the row. End the row with SC2TOG across the last 2 stitches, pulling through on the last step of the stitch with Soft Peach.

ROW 4 (BERRY ROW): SC2TOG across the first two stitches. *Work one Berry Stitch in the next stitch. Work 1 SC in the next stitch. Repeat from * to the middle stitch of the 3 SC that makes the peak. Work "SC, Berry, SC" in middle stitch. Then continue the pattern of alternating the Berry Stitch and SC until you reach the bottom valley. Work Berry Stitch, skip two stitches, work Berry Stitch and then continue the pattern. End the row with SC2TOG.

Tip: The only time where you won't put a SC in between the Berry Stitch is the bottom of the valleys where you skip two stitches—I counted the skipped stitches as my SC in between the berries, so you'll work a Berry Stitch, skip two stitches, then crochet another Berry. Then you'll resume alternating the Berry Stitch with SC.

You are working this row exactly the same as rows 2 and 3, but you are substituting every other SC for a Berry Stitch (except in the valleys where you have two berries next to each other). When you reach the end of the row, SC2TOG and pull through with White.

REPEAT ROWS 1 - 4 until the blanket measures appx. 38 inches in length. Weave in ends with a tapestry needle.

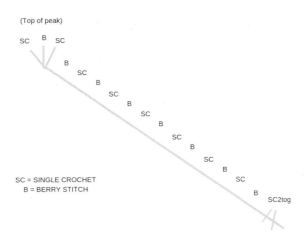

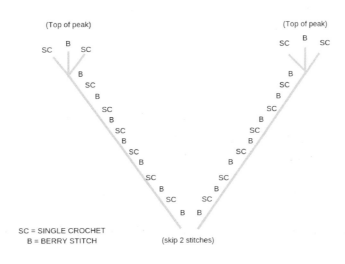

CHECKERBOARD LINES BABY BLANKET

By Hannah

MATERIALS

YARN   Red Heart Soft
(100% acrylic, 283 g/10 oz, 469 m/513 yds)
4 skeins Seafoam
2 skeins White

HOOK   Size I, 5.50mm hook

TOOLS   Tapestry needle, Scissors

SIZE   Finished size: 32 in x 35 in
Gauge: 4 in = 16 rows and 12 stitches

STITCHES

SINGLE CROCHET (SC): Insert your hook, yarn over (YO) and pull up a loop, YO and pull through both loops.

HERRINGBONE HALF DOUBLE CROCHET (HHDC): YO, insert your hook, YO and pull up a loop and pull directly through first loop on hook. Then YO and pull through remaining loops on hook.

PATTERN

CHAIN 112 with Seafoam. (Pattern repeat is any multiple of 10, plus 2.)

ROW 1: Work 1 HHDC in the 3rd chain from the hook. HHDC in each chain across the row. CH 2 and turn.

ROW 2: HHDC in each stitch across the row. *(The turning chain does not count as a stitch, so when you start a new row, insert your hook directly into the top of the last stitch of the previous row.)* When you reach the end of row 2, pull through with White. Don't cut the Seafoam. CH 1 and turn.

ROW 3: Work 1 SC in each of the next 10 stitches with White, carrying the Seafoam along the row and crocheting over it as you go. On the 10th stitch, pull through with Seafoam before you finish the stitch. Then work 1 SC in each of the next 10 stitches with Seafoam and carry White along the row and crochet over it. Continue switching between Seafoam and White every 10 stitches, always carrying whichever yarn you aren't using along the row and working over it. When you reach the end of the row, CH 1 and turn with White.

Tip: The best way to keep your yarn from getting twisted while carrying yarn is to always keep one color to the front and one to the back. For this blanket I chose to keep White to the front—so every time I switched from White to Seafoam, I folded my White yarn over the top of my work first, and then pulled through with Seafoam. And whenever I stopped using Seafoam, I just left it to the back and then pulled through with White.

ROW 4: Repeat row 3. When you reach the end of the row, pull through with Seafoam on the last stitch and CH 2 and turn. Don't cut the White—leave it so you can pick it back up and carry it up the edge when you get back to that side of the blanket.

ROWS 5 - 6: HHDC in each stitch across the row in Seafoam. At the end of row 5, CH 2 and turn. At the end of row 6, pull through White, then CH 1 and turn.

ROWS 7 - 8: Repeat rows 3 and 4.

ROWS 9 - 10: HHDC in each stitch across the row with Seafoam. CH 2 and turn. At the end of row 10, pull through White, then CH 1 and turn.

ROWS 11 - 12: Repeat rows 3 and 4.

ROWS 13 - 14: HHDC in each stitch across the row in Seafoam. At the end of row 13, CH 2 and turn. At the end of row 14, CH 1 and turn.

ROW 15: SC in each of the next 10 stitches in Seafoam, carrying White up the side from below and crocheting over it. On the 10th stitch, pull through White. SC in each of the next 10 stitches with White, carrying Seafoam along and working over it. Continue switching between Seafoam and White every 10 stitches, always carrying whichever yarn you aren't using along the row. At the end of the row CH 1 and turn.

ROW 16: Repeat row 15. At the end of the row, CH 2 and turn.

ROWS 17 - 18: HHDC in each stitch across the row with Seafoam. At the end of row 17, CH 2 and turn. At the end of row 18, CH 1 and turn.

ROWS 19 - 20: Repeat rows 15 - 16.

ROWS 21 - 22: HHDC in each stitch across the row in Seafoam. At the end of row 21, CH 2 and turn. At the end of row 22, CH 1 and turn.

ROWS 23 - 24: Repeat rows 15 - 16.

ROWS 25 - 26: HHDC in each stitch across the row in Seafoam. At the end of row 25, CH 2 and turn. At the end of row 26, pull through white White, CH 1 and turn.

REPEAT ROWS 3 - 26 until you reach your desired length, ending your blanket with 2 rows of HHDC in Seafoam.

I finished my blanket with 112 rows total.

BORDER

Weave in any ends with a tapestry needle.

ROUND 1: With Seafoam, pull up a loop in any corner and CH 1. SC around the blanket, working 3 SCs into each corner. When you reach the corner you started with, slip stitch into the starting stitch, then chain 2 and turn.

ROUND 2: Work one HHDC in each stitch around the blanket, and 3 HHDCs in each corner stitch. When you reach the corner you started with, slip stitch into the starting stitch, then chain 2 and turn.

ROUND 3: Work one HHDC in each stitch around the blanket, and 3 HHDCs in each corner stitch. When you reach the corner you started with, slip stitch into the corner and tie off.

If you'd like to add finishing touches to your blanket, lay it out flat on a towel or foam blocking boards if you have them. Use a spray bottle with water to dampen the blanket. Press the blanket into straight lines, massaging the stitches and adjusting your tension. Pin with straight pins to let it dry.

DAINTY STRIPES BABY BLANKET

By Tiffany

MATERIALS

YARN   Bernat Softee Baby
(100% acrylic, 140g 5 oz, 331 m/362 yds)
4 skeins White
1 skein Pumpkin
1 skein Soft Peach

HOOK   Size G, 4.00mm hook

TOOLS   Tapestry needle, Scissors

SIZE   Finished size: 29 in x 31 in
Gauge: 4 in = 22 stitches and 18 rows

STITCHES

PUFF STITCH: Yarn over (YO), insert hook into designated space, YO and pull up a loop, *YO, insert hook into same space, YO and pull up a loop. Repeat one more time from *. Then, YO and pull through all loops on hook.

SINGLE CROCHET (SC): Insert your hook, yarn over (YO) and pull up a loop, YO and pull through both loops on your hook.

DOUBLE CROCHET (DC): YO, insert your hook, YO and pull up a loop, YO, pull through two loops, YO, pull through remaining two loops on your hook.

PATTERN

CHAIN 141 with White. (Pattern repeat is any multiple of 3.)

ROW 1: In the 2nd chain from the hook, work "SC, CH, DC", *skip 2 chains, work "SC, CH, DC" in the next chain. Repeat from * to the end of the row and until you have 1 remaining chain space. Work 1 SC in the last remaining chain space. CH 1 and turn.

ROW 2: "SC, CH, DC" in the top of the first SC of the row below. *Skip over the next two stitches. Work "SC, CH, DC" into the SC stitch of the row below. Repeat from * ending the row with 1 SC in the very last stitch, CH 1 and turn.

ROWS 3 - 4: Repeat row 2. Pull through with Soft Peach on the last SC of row 4, CH 1 and turn. (Do not cut the White, bring it around the end of your work and crochet over it as you go.)

ROW 5 (PUFF ROW): "SC, Puff, DC" in the top of the SC of the row below. *Skip over the next two stitches. Work "SC, Puff, DC" into the SC of the row below. Repeat from * ending the row with 1 SC in the very last stitch and pulling through with White on the last step of the stitch. Cut the Soft Peach. CH 1 and turn.

ROWS 6 - 10: Repeat row 2 with White. CH 1 and turn. At the end of the 5th row, pull through with Pumpkin. (Leave the White behind, you don't need to crochet over it and bring it along this time.)

ROW 11: Repeat row 5 with Pumpkin. At the end of the row, pull through with Soft Peach.

ROW 12: Repeat row 5 with Soft Peach. (You may choose to carry the Pumpkin along with you and crochet over it, or cut and weave in the end later.) At the end of the row, pull through with Pumpkin.

ROW 13: Repeat row 5 with Soft Peach. (You may also pull the White up from two rows below and crochet over it, or cut and weave in the tail later.)

ROWS 14 - 18: Repeat row 2 with White.

ROW 19: Repeat row 5 with Soft Peach. (You may choose to carry the White along the row, or cut and weave the tail in later.)

ROWS 20 - 30: Repeat row 2 with White. At the end of row 30, pull through with Pumpkin.

ROW 31: Repeat row 5 with Pumpkin. (You may crochet over the White or cut and weave in later.)

ROWS 32 - 42: Repeat row 2 with White. At the end of row 42, pull through with Soft Peach.

ROW 43: Repeat row 5 with Soft Peach.

REPEAT ROWS 32 - 43 three more times. (You will have a total of 4 puff rows of Soft Peach.)

WORK 11 ROWS OF WHITE THEN REPEAT THE INSTRUCTIONS BACKWARD FROM ROW 31 THROUGH ROW 1.

You are mirroring the start of the blanket so both ends look the same.

BORDER

Tie off and weave in all ends.

Start in the corner as if you chained and turned your work.

With White, work across the row using the "SC, CH 1, DC" combo into the SC spaces. When you get to the corner, work a combo into the corner space. When working down the sides, work one combo per two rows. (You should be able to see that there is a slightly larger hole, work into that space.)

Continue working around the entire blanket and slip stitch to your beginning stitch. Tie off and weave in the ends.

If you'd like to add finishing touches to your blanket, lay it out flat on a towel or foam blocking boards if you have them. Use a spray bottle with water to dampen the blanket. Press the blanket into straight lines, massaging the stitches and adjusting your tension. Pin with straight pins to let it dry.

POLKA DOT LINES BABY BLANKET

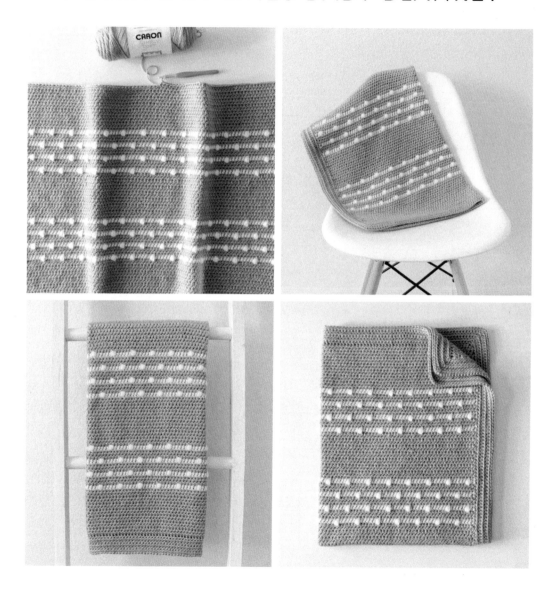

By Hannah

MATERIALS

YARN   Caron Simply Soft
(100% acrylic, 170 g/6 oz, 288 m/315 yds)
4 skeins Victorian Rose
1 skein White

HOOK   Size H, 5.00mm hook

TOOLS   Tapestry needle, Scissors

SIZE   Finished size: 31 in x 41 in
Gauge: 4 in = 16 stitches and 12 rows

STITCHES

WIDE HALF DOUBLE CROCHET (WHDC): YO (yarn over) and insert your hook in between the posts of the row below, YO and pull up a loop, YO, pull through all loops on hook.

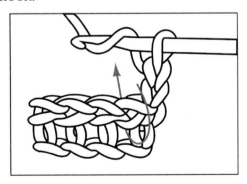

PUFF STITCH: *YO, insert your hook into designated space, YO and pull up a loop. Repeat from * 4 more times (inserting your hook into the same space). Then YO and pull through all the loops on your hook.

FRONT TWO LOOP HALF DOUBLE CROCHET (F2LHDC): YO, insert your hook up through the front two loops of the next stitch, YO and pull up a loop. YO and pull through all three loops on hook.

PATTERN

CHAIN 97 with Victorian Rose. (Pattern repeat is any multiple of 6, plus 1.)

ROW 1: Starting in the 3rd chain from the hook, work 1 HDC. 1 HDC in each chain across the row. When you reach the end, CH 2 and turn.

ROWS 2 - 15: Work 1 WHDC in each space between the stitches across the row. (Your last stitch will be between the turning chain and the last stitch.) CH 2 and turn. On row 15, pull through with White on the last stitch (you should have 3 loops on your hook when you pull through). CH 2 with and turn.

ROW 16: With White, work *1 WHDC in each of the next 5 spaces, 1 puff stitch in the next space. Repeat from * across the row and end with 1 WHDC in each of the last 5 spaces. On the last stitch of the row, pull through with Victorian Rose. CH 2 and turn.

ROWS 17 - 19: With Victorian Rose, work 1 WHDC in each space across the row. CH 2 and turn. On the last stitch of row 19, pull through with White. CH 2 and turn.

Tip: Treat the puff stitches like they are normal WHDC and work a stitch on either side of the puffs.

ROW 20: With White, work 1 WHDC in each of the first 2 spaces. Work 1 puff stitch. *Work 1 WHDC in each of the next 5 spaces, then work 1 puff stitch. Repeat from * across the row and end with a WHDC in each of the last two spaces. Pull through with Victorian Rose on the last stitch. CH 2 and turn.

ROWS 21 - 23: With Victorian Rose, work 1 WHDC in each space across the row. CH 2 and turn. On the last stitch of row 23, pull through with White. CH 2 and turn.

ROW 24: Repeat row 16 with White.

ROWS 25 - 27: With Victorian Rose, work 1 WHDC in each space across the row. CH 2 and turn. On the last stitch of row 27, pull through with White. CH 2 and turn.

ROW 28: Repeat row 20 with White.

ROWS 29 - 43: Work 1 WHDC in each space across the row, CH 2 and turn.

REPEAT ROWS 16 - 43 until you have four sets of white stripes and you end with 15 rows of Victorian Rose.

Weave in all ends with a tapestry needle.

BORDER

ROUND 1: To start the border, pull up a loop in any corner with Victorian Rose and CH 2. Work one regular HDC per stitch around the entire blanket, working 3 HDCs into each corner space. When returning to the starting corner, work two HDCs and slip stitch to the starting chain 2.
CH 2 and turn.

ROUND 2: Work one F2LHDC per stitch around the entire blanket, working 3 stitches in each corner. When returning to the starting corner, work two F2LHDCs and slip stitch to the starting chain 2. CH 2 and turn.

ROUNDS 3 - 4: Repeat row 2. After the 4th round, slip stitch into final space and tie off and weave in the ends.

If you'd like to add finishing touches to your blanket, lay it out flat on a towel or foam blocking boards if you have them. Use a spray bottle with water to dampen the blanket. Press the blanket into straight lines, massaging the stitches and adjusting your tension. Pin with straight pins and let it dry.

SUMMERTIME STRIPES BABY BLANKET

By Tiffany

MATERIALS

YARN   Caron Simply Soft
(100% acrylic, 170 g/6 oz, 288 m 315 yds)
2 skeins White
1 skein Persimmon
1 skein Sunshine
1 skein Light Country Blue

HOOK   Size H, 5.00mm hook

TOOLS   Tapestry needle, Scissors

SIZE   Finished size: 31 in x 34 in
Gauge: 4 in = 17 stitches and 12 rows

STITCHES

SINGLE CROCHET (SC): Insert your hook, yarn over (YO) and pull up a loop, YO and pull through both loops.

HERRINGBONE HALF DOUBLE CROCHET (HHDC): YO, insert your hook, YO, pull up a loop and pull directly through first loop on hook. Then YO and pull through remaining loops on hook.

HALF DOUBLE CROCHET (HDC): YO, insert your hook, YO and pull up a loop, YO, pull through three loops.

DOUBLE CROCHET (DC): YO, insert your hook, YO and pull up a loop, YO, pull through two loops, YO, pull through last two loops.

HALF DOUBLE CROCHET (HDC) CLUSTER: YO, insert your hook into the stitch you just worked with a HDC, then YO and pull a loop, then YO again, insert your hook into the next unworked stitch, YO and pull a loop, YO and pull through all loops left on the hook.

PATTERN

CHAIN 120 with White.

ROW 1: HHDC into the 3rd chain from the hook. HHDC into each chain across. CH 1 and turn.

ROWS 2 - 10: HHDC into each stitch across the row, CH 1 and turn.

ROW 11: Work 1 HDC into the 1st stitch from the row below. *Work HDC Cluster into each stitch across by yarning over and inserting your hook into the stitch you just worked with a HDC, then yarning over and pulling a loop back through, then yarn over again, insert your hook into the next unworked stitch, yarn over and pull a loop back through, yarn over and pull through all loops left on the hook. Repeat across the row from *. Before finishing the last step of the last stitch, pull through with the color Persimmon. CH 1 and turn.

ROWS 12 - 21: Repeat the instructions for rows 2 - 10 with Persimmon. (10 rows)

ROW 22: Work one row of HDC Clusters as explained above.

Continue the rest of the blanket as rows 12 - 22 using the color changes in this order: Persimmon, Sunshine, Light Country Blue, and White. Each cluster row is made with White.

Repeat the colors again and end with 10 rows of White.

Do not tie off, but do weave in all the ends before continuing with the border.

BORDER

After weaving in all the ends, chain one and turn. Work 1 DC into each stitch, 3 DC into each corner, and work 1 DC per row down the sides of the blanket. Join with a slip stitch at the end of the round to the starting DC. CH 1 and turn.

Work 1 HDC into the first stitch. Work HDC cluster across two stitches around the entire blanket. Slip stitch to join with the beginning HDC. CH 1 and turn.

SC into each HDC cluster stitch, work 3 SC into each corner HDC cluster, join with a slip stitch at the end of the round, tie off and weave in the end.

If you'd like to add finishing touches to your blanket, lay it out flat on a towel or foam blocking boards if you have them. Use a spray bottle with water to dampen the blanket. Press the blanket into straight lines, massaging the stitches and adjusting your tension. Pin with straight pins to let it dry.

TEAL GINGHAM BABY BLANKET

By Tiffany

MATERIALS

YARN   Paton's Canadiana
(100% Acrylic, 100 g/3.5 oz, 187 m/205 yds)
2 skeins Winter White
2 skeins Medium Teal
4 skeins Pale Teal

HOOK   Size I, 5.50mm hook

TOOLS   Tapestry needle, Scissors

SIZE   Finished blanket size: 34 in x 34 in
Gauge: 4 in = 16 stitches and 8 rows

STITCHES

HERRINGBONE DOUBLE CROCHET (HBDC): Yarn over (YO), insert your hook, YO and pull back through the stitch, AND through the first loop on your hook. Then, YO and pull through ONE loop of the hook. Then, YO and pull through the remaining two loops on your hook.

HERRINGBONE HALF DOUBLE CROCHET (HHDC): YO, insert your hook, YO and pull back through stitch AND through first loop on hook, YO and pull through both remaining loops on the hook.

PATTERN

CHAIN 107 with Pale Teal. (Pattern repeat is any odd number times 5, plus 2.)

ROW 1: Work 1 Herringbone DC (HBDC) in the 3rd chain from the hook. Work 1 HBDC in each of the next 4 chains, pulling through on the last step of the stitch with Winter White. Work 1 HBDC in each of the next 5 chains, crocheting over and carrying along Pale Teal, then pull Pale Teal through on the last step of the 5th HBDC. Continue across the chain switching colors every 5 stitches. CH 2 and turn at the end of the row, wrapping the Winter White around the end and crocheting over it for the next row.

ROWS 2 - 4: Continue repeating the instructions in row 1, alternating the colors every 5 stitches. The turning chain does not count as a stitch. On the last stitch in row 4, pull through with Medium Teal and leave the Winter White behind. (You may cut the White to weave in later, or choose to carry Winter White up the side of the blanket if you don't mind seeing bits of white in your border.)

ROWS 5 - 8: Work 1 HBDC in each of the first 5 stitches with Medium Teal, carrying the Pale Teal along, crocheting over it, and changing to Pale Teal for the next 5 stitches. Repeat these color changes across the row as before. CH 2 and turn.

ROWS 9 - 68: Continue switching the colors as explained in previous rows. You will finish with 17 blocks of color high. (Or do more, if you want your blanket more oblong, just finish on a Pale Teal, Winter White row to match the starting rows.)

BORDER

Weave in all the ends before starting the border.

ROUND 1: Choose any corner and pull up a loop and CH 2 with Medium Teal. Work each stitch across with HBDC. Work 3 HBDC in each corner. Work HBDC as evenly as possible down the sides of your blanket. A rough guide is 2 HBDC around the turning chains and 1 HBDC per the rows that start with HBDC, but that is just a rough guide. If your sides are puckering, it's either too many, or too few.

ROUND 2: Do not join the rounds, just finish the starting corner with 3 HBDC then continue on in the same directions changing your stitch to HHDC. Work 3 HHDC into each corner. Don't join these rounds and don't turn. Continue for one more round of HHDC.

Join with a slip stitch and weave in the ends.

If you'd like to add finishing touches to your blanket, lay it out flat on a towel or foam blocking boards if you have them. Use a spray bottle with water to dampen the blanket. Press the blanket into straight lines, massaging the stitches and adjusting your tension. Pin with straight pins to let it dry.

BOBBLE LINES BABY BLANKET

By Hannah

MATERIALS

YARN   Bernat Softee Baby
             (100% acrylic, 140g/5 oz, 331 m/362 yds)
             4 skeins White
             1 skein Soft Red
             1 skein Soft Peach
             1 skein Aqua
             1 skein Navy

HOOK   Size H, 5.00mm hook

TOOLS   Tapestry needle, Scissors

SIZE   Finished size: 35 in x 35 in
             Gauge: 4 in = 17 stitches and 13 rows

STITCHES

SINGLE CROCHET (SC): Insert your hook, yarn over (YO) and pull up a loop, YO and pull through both loops on your hook.

HERRINGBONE HALF DOUBLE CROCHET (HHDC): YO, insert your hook, YO, pull up a loop and pull directly through the first loop on your hook. YO and pull through both loops on your hook.

DOUBLE CROCHET (DC): YO, insert your hook, YO and pull up a loop, YO, pull through two loops, YO, pull through remaining two loops on your hook.

FRONT AND BACK POST DOUBLE CROCHET (FPDC & BPDC): A front post double crochet means you insert your hook from front to back around the post of the next DC and work a DC. A back post double crochet means you insert your hook from back to front around the post of the next DC and work a DC.

DOUBLE CROCHET 5 TOGETHER (DC5TOG) BOBBLE: YO, insert your hook, YO and pull up a loop, YO and pull through 2 loops. Then, *YO again, insert your hook into the same space, YO and pull up a loop, YO and pull through 2 loops. Repeat from * 3 more times until you have 6 loops on your hook. Then YO and pull through all 6 loops on your hook.

PATTERN

CHAIN 120 with White. (The pattern repeat is a multiple of 7, plus 8.)

ROW 1: Work 1 HHDC in the 3rd chain from the hook. Work 1 HHDC in each chain to the end of the row. CH 2 and turn.

ROWS 2 - 5: Work 1 HHDC in each stitch across the row. CH 2 and turn. *(The chain 2 from the row below does not count as a stitch, so at the beginning of each row you'll want to insert your hook directly into the first stitch, and then you don't have to go into the turning chain at the end of the row.)*

When you reach the end of row 5, pull through with Navy on the last stitch, when you still have two loops left on your hook. Cut the White yarn, leaving a tail long enough to weave in later. CH 1 with Navy and turn.

ROW 6: *SC in each of the next 6 stitches, then work 1 DC5TOG bobble in the next stitch. Repeat from * across the row, ending with one SC in each of the last 6 stitches. On the last SC, pull through with White. Cut the Navy and leave a tail long enough to weave in later. CH 2 with White and turn.

ROWS 7 - 11: Work 1 HHDC in each stitch across the row, chaining 2 and turning at the end of the first four rows. At the end of the last row, pull through with Soft Peach, and CH 1 and turn.

ROW 12: Repeat row 6 with Soft Peach.

ROWS 13 - 17: Work 1 HHDC with White in each stitch across the row, chaining 2 and turning at the end of the first four rows. At the end of the last row, pull through with Aqua, and CH 1 and turn.

ROW 18: Repeat row 6 with Aqua.

ROWS 19 - 23: Work one HHDC with White in each stitch across the row, chaining 2 and turning at the end of the first four rows. At the end of the last row, pull through with Soft Red, and CH 1 and turn.

ROW 24: Repeat row 6 with Soft Red.

ROWS 25 - 29: Work one HHDC in White in each stitch across the row, chaining 2 and turning at the end of the first four rows. At the end of the last row, pull through with Navy, and CH 1 and turn.

REPEAT ROWS 6 THROUGH 29 for the rest of the blanket until you reach your desired length and end with 5 rows of HHDC in White. I ended up with 16 bobble rows when my blanket was the length I wanted.

BORDER

ROUND 1: With White, pull up a loop in any corner and CH 3. DC as evenly as possible around the entire blanket, working 3 DCs into each corner stitch.

ROUND 2: When you reach the corner you started with, do not join or turn. Work 3 DCs into the corner, then continuing in the same direction, alternate front and back post double crochet (FPDC & BPDC) around each DC. When you get to the corners of this row, you will want to continue the pattern of alternating FPDC and BPDC, but you will work 3 stitches around the corner post.

So, for example, if you get to the corner post and you are supposed to work a FPDC, then work a FPDC, a BPDC, and a FPDC all around that corner post. Then in the next stitch you would continue the alternating pattern, working the opposite of whichever stitch you just used. Just remember that you are always alternating FPDC and BPDC around the whole blanket, you just happen to be working three of those stitches around the same post when you are working the corners.

ROUND 3: When you finish round 2, work 3 alternating FPDC/BPDC into the corner you started with. Do not join or turn. Continuing around, repeat round 2. Always match your post double crochets so that they are popping out in the same direction as the previous row.

ROUNDS 4 - 6: Repeat round 3.

ROUND 7: After my last row of front/back post DCs, I worked one round of SC in each stitch around the blanket, working 3 SCs into each of the corners. When I reached the corner I started with, I worked 3 SCs into the corner, then slip stitched into the starting stitch and tied off.

COUNTRY BLUE SHADES BABY BLANKET

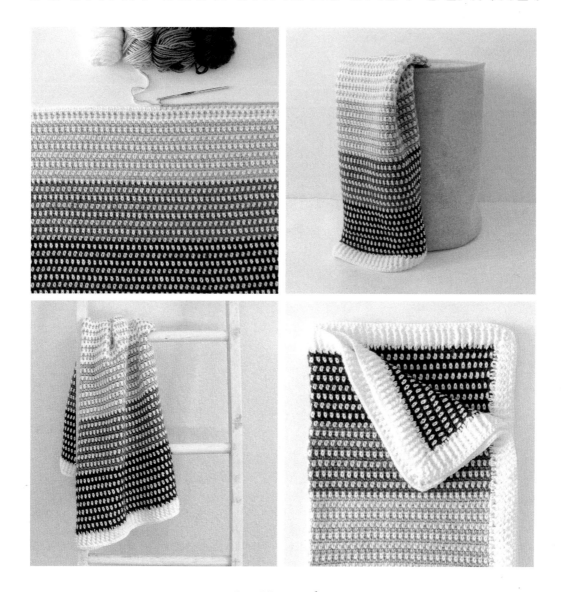

By Hannah

MATERIALS

YARN   Caron Simply Soft
(100% acrylic, 170 g 6 oz, 288 m/315 yds)
2 skeins White
1 skein Dark Country Blue
1 skein Country Blue
1 skein Light Country Blue

HOOK   Size H, 5.00mm hook

TOOLS   Tapestry needle, Scissors

SIZE   Finished size: 29 in x 42 in
Gauge: 4 in = 10 stitches and 16 rows

STITCHES

SINGLE CROCHET (SC): Insert your hook, yarn over (YO) and pull up a loop, YO and pull through both loops on your hook.

DOUBLE CROCHET (DC): YO, insert your hook, YO and pull up a loop, YO, pull through two loops, YO, pull through remaining two loops on your hook.

FRONT AND BACK POST DOUBLE CROCHET (FPDC & BPDC): A front post double crochet means you insert your hook from front to back around the post of the next DC and work a DC. A back post double crochet means you insert your hook from back to front around the post of the next DC and work a DC.

MOSS STITCH: (explained in pattern)

PATTERN

CHAIN 120 (or any even number) with Dark Country Blue.

ROW 1: Start in the 4th chain from the hook and SC, CH 1. *Skip one chain, then SC, CH 1 in the next chain. Repeat from * to the end of the row. Work 1 SC into the last chain. CH 2 and turn.

What I'm telling you to do is chain one after you make that first single crochet, skip the next chain, and single crochet into the next one, then chain one. Repeat working a single crochet, chain one, skip over one chain until you get to the end of the row and finish with a SC and chain 2. This is called the Moss Stitch.

ROW 2: Skip the first stitch, then SC, CH 1 in the chain 1 space of the row below. *Skip one chain, then SC, CH 1 in the next space (Moss Stitch). Repeat from * to the end, working your final SC into the space between the last SC and turning chain. On the last SC of row 2, pull through with White (you should have two loops on your hook when you pull through). CH 2 with White and turn. Don't cut the Blue.

ROW 3: Pull the Blue around to the back and work the Moss Stitch (repeat row 2) across the row with White, laying the Blue across the top of the row and crocheting over it as you work. When you reach the end of the row, pull through with Blue. CH 2 and turn. Don't cut the White yarn.

ROWS 4 - 5: Work 2 rows of the Moss Stitch in Dark Country Blue. On these rows, you are *not* crocheting over the White yarn. Instead you will be picking it back up when you finish your second row of Dark Country Blue and carry it up the side of your work. On the last stitch of row 5, pull through with White. Then CH 2 and turn. Don't cut the Blue yarn.

REPEAT ROWS 3 - 5 for the rest of the blanket noting the color changes explained further.

DARK COUNTRY BLUE SECTION: 16 rows of Dark Country Blue, with a row of White in between every two rows of Blue. After you have 16 rows of Dark Country Blue, repeat row 3 and work one row of White, but don't carry the Dark Country Blue. Instead, cut the Blue and leave a tail long enough to weave in later.

COUNTRY BLUE SECTION: At the end of the White row, pull through with Country Blue and work two rows of Country Blue in the Moss Stitch. Pull through with White at the end of the second row and repeat rows 3 through 5 until you have 14 rows of Country Blue, with a row of White in between every two rows of Blue. After you have 14 rows of Country Blue, repeat row 3 and work one row of White, but don't carry the Country Blue. Instead, cut the Country Blue and leave a tail long enough to weave in later.

LIGHT COUNTRY BLUE SECTION: At the end of the White row, pull through with Light Country Blue and work two rows of Light Country Blue in the Moss Stitch. Pull through with White at the end of the second row and repeat rows 3 through 5 until you have 14 rows of Light Country Blue, with a row of White in between every two rows of Light Country Blue. After you have 14 rows of Light Country Blue, repeat row 3 and work one row of White, but don't carry the Light Country Blue. Don't cut the Light Country Blue.

WHITE SECTION: You are now going to be making the White section with Light Country Blue stripes instead of a blue section with white stripes, so work one more row of White, and then pick up the Light Country Blue from the side and work one row of Light Country Blue and carry the White yarn behind. Then work 2 rows of White, and leave the Light Country Blue behind. Repeat rows 3 through 5 (with opposite colors) until you have 14 rows of White, with one row of Light Country Blue in between every two rows of White.

After you complete the White section, finish the blanket by reversing the order you did the sections at the beginning—so repeat the Light Country Blue section, then the Country Blue section, then end with the Dark Country Blue section.

BORDER

ROUND 1: With White, pull up a loop in any corner and CH 1. Work one SC, CH 1 in every other space around the blanket, working three SCs into the corners.

ROUND 2: When you reach the beginning SC, do not join or turn. Work 1 DC in each SC and CH 1 space around the entire blanket, and work 3 DCs into each corner stitch.

ROUND 3: When you reach the first DC of the round, work 3 DCs into the corner, then go around the blanket again in the same direction, this time alternating front and back post double crochet (FPDC & BPDC). When you get to the corners of this row, you will want to continue the pattern of alternating FPDC and BPDC, but you will work 3 stitches around the corner post.

So, for example, if you get to the corner post and you are supposed to work a FPDC, then work a FPDC, a BPDC, and a FPDC all around that corner post. Then in the next stitch you would continue the alternating pattern, working the opposite of whichever stitch you just used. Just remember that you are always alternating FPDC and BPDC around the whole blanket, you just happen to be working three of those stitches around the same post when you are working the corners.

ROUND 4: When you finish round 3, work 3 alternating FPDC/BPDC into the corner you started with and repeat round 3 around the blanket. Always match your post double crochets so that they are poking out in the same direction as the previous row.

ROUNDS 5 - 6: Repeat round 3. When you reach the corner you stared with, slip stitch into the corner and tie off.

BOXED BLOCK BABY BLANKET

By Tiffany

MATERIALS

YARN   Caron Simply Soft
(100% acrylic, 170 g/6 oz, 288 m/315 yds)
3 skeins Off White
1 skein Gold
1 skein Gray Heather
1 skein Soft Blue

HOOK   Size H, 5.00mm hook

TOOLS   Tapestry needle, Scissors

SIZE   Finished size: 36 in x 45 in
Gauge: 4 in = 16 stitches and 8 rows

STITCHES

SINGLE CROCHET (SC): Insert your hook, yarn over (YO) and pull up a loop, YO and pull through both loops on your hook.

DOUBLE CROCHET (DC): YO, insert your hook, YO and pull up a loop, YO, pull through two loops, YO, pull through remaining two loops on your hook.

FRONT AND BACK POST DOUBLE CROCHET (FPDC & BPDC): A front post double crochet means you insert your hook from front to back around the post of the next DC and work a DC. A back post double crochet means you insert your hook from back to front around the post of the next DC and work a DC.

PATTERN

CHAIN 103 with Off White. (Pattern repeat is a multiple of 5, plus 3.)

ROW 1: SC in the 2nd chain from the hook and in each stitch across. CH 1 and turn.

ROW 2: *Work 1 SC in each of the next two stitches, CH 3, skip the next three stitches, 1 SC in each of the next two stitches. Repeat from * to the end. Your last two stitches will be 1 SC in each of the last two spaces. CH 3 and turn.

ROW 3: Skip over the first 2 stitches and work 5 DC into the CH 3 space. Work 5 DC into each chain 3 space across the row. End with one DC in the last SC of the row below. CH 1 and turn.

ROW 4: Work 1 SC into each of the first two DC, *CH 3, skip over the next 3 DC, work 1 SC in each of the next 2 DC, Repeat from * across the row; your last two stitches will be one SC in each of the last two spaces.

ROW 5: Repeat Row 3.

ROW 6 TO THE END OF THE BLANKET: Repeat rows 4 and 3 referring to the color changes described below:

I started with the Off White and used it for the first 3 "boxes" changing to gray when I worked the SC /chain 3 row. I worked back across, making the boxes, then changed colors to Soft Blue. (I did not cut the Gray. To save time and eliminate a number of ends needing to be woven in, I carried the yarn up the sides in this color section.) I worked one set of "boxes" with the Soft Blue, changed to Gold for one set, back to Soft Blue, and then final color change back to Gray.

Then, I worked 5 sets of "boxes" in Off White before repeating the color section again. I have 4 sets of color sections with 5 sets of Off White, with the exception being that the first blocks of Off White are only 3 rows.

Maybe this will make it more clear:

3 Off White, 5 colors, 5 Off White, 5 colors, 5 Off White, 5 colors, 5 Off White, 5 colors, 3 Off White

Finish the last row by working a SC into every DC. (This will mirror the starting of the blanket.)

Weave in all ends before you start the border.

BORDER

ROUND 1: With Off White, pull up a loop in any corner and chain 3. DC around the entire blanket, working 3 DCs into each corner stitch.

ROUND 2: When you reach the corner you started with, work 3 DCs into the corner, then go around the blanket again in the same direction, this time alternating front and back post double crochet (FPDC & BPDC). When you get to the corners of this row, you will want to continue the pattern of alternating FPDC and BPDC, but you will work 3 stitches around the corner post.

So, for example, if you get to the corner post and you are supposed to work a FPDC, then work a FPDC, a BPDC, and a FPDC all around that corner post. Then in the next stitch you would continue the alternating pattern, working the opposite of whichever stitch you just used. Just remember that you are always alternating FPDC and BPDC around the whole blanket, you just happen to be working three of those stitches around the same post when you are working the corners.

ROUND 3: When you finish round 2, work 3 alternating FPDC/BPDC into the corner you started with and repeat round 2 around the blanket. Always match your post double crochets so that they are popping out in the same direction as the previous row.

ROUNDS 4 - 5: Repeat round 3. When you reach the starting corner after round 5, slip stitch into the corner and tie off.

If you'd like to add finishing touches to your blanket, lay it out flat on a towel or foam blocking boards if you have them. Use a spray bottle with water to dampen the blanket. Press the blanket into straight lines, massaging the stitches and adjusting your tension. Pin with straight pins and let it dry.

BOHO COLOR BLOCK BABY BLANKET

By Hannah

MATERIALS

YARN   Caron Simply Soft
(100% acrylic, 170 g/6 oz, 288 m/315 yds)
1 skein White
1 skein Victorian Rose
1 skein Soft Green
1 skein Light Country Peach

HOOK   Size H, 5.00mm hook

TOOLS   Tapestry needle, Scissors

SIZE   Finished size: 30 in x 40 in
Gauge: 4 in = 10 stitches and 12 rows

STITCHES

SINGLE CROCHET (SC): Insert your hook, yarn over (YO) and pull up a loop, YO and pull through both loops on your hook.

MODIFIED DAISY STITCH: (explained in pattern)

PATTERN

CHAIN 121 (or any odd number) with Victorian Rose.

ROW 1: Yarn over (YO) and pull up a loop in the 2nd chain from the hook, YO and pull up a loop in the 3rd chain from the hook. Skip over the next (4th) chain, then YO and insert your hook into the next (5th) chain and pull up a loop. YO and pull through all seven loops on your hook. CH 1.

*YO and insert your hook into the CH 1 space and pull up a loop. YO and insert your hook into the last chain space you worked into and pull up a loop. Skip over the next chain, then YO and insert your hook into the next chain and pull up a loop. YO and pull through all 7 loops. CH 1. Repeat from * to the end of the row. CH 3 and turn. (The first of these chains will count as the one that closes the loop.)

ROW 2: YO and work into the 2nd chain from the hook and pull up a loop, insert your hook into the 3rd chain from the hook and pull up a loop, skip the next stitch, YO and pull up a loop in the next space. YO and pull through all 7 loops. CH 1.

*YO and insert your hook into the chain space and pull up a loop, YO and insert your hook into the next space and pull up a loop, skip over one stitch, YO and insert your hook into the next space and pull up a loop. YO and pull through all loops on your hook. Repeat from * across ending with the last leg of the last stitch in the turning chain, CH 3 and turn (the first of these turning chains counting as the one that closes the loop).

REPEAT ROW 2 for the rest of the blanket.

When changing colors, you'll want to pull through with the new color on the last stitch of the row when you have 7 loops on your hook. Then you'll CH 3 with the new color and turn.

COLOR CHANGES:

10 rows Victorian Rose, 10 rows Light Country Peach, 10 rows Soft Green, 10 rows White, 10 rows Soft Green, 10 rows Light Country Peach, 10 rows Victorian Rose

BORDER

When I finished the blanket, I decided to add a simple thin White border before adding the tassels. To add the border, pull up a loop in any corner and CH one, then work a SC plus CH 1 in every other stitch (or between the posts on the sides) around the whole blanket, working 3 SCs into the corners.

When you reach the corner you started with, work 1 round of SC in every other stitch around the blanket, again working 3 SCs into the corners. When you get back to where you started, slip stitch into the corner and tie off.

TASSELS

Cut several nine inch pieces of yarn.

Take three to four pieces of yarn (depending on how thick you want your tassels; for this blanket I used four) and fold them in half. Insert the folded end into the chain space above the last row. You can use your fingers or a large crochet hook to do this. Pull the ends through the loop and pull tight to make a knot.

You can space your tassels out however far apart you'd like and you can also make the tassels longer by using a bigger notebook, or trim them down if you want them to be shorter.

EVEN SQUARES BABY BLANKET

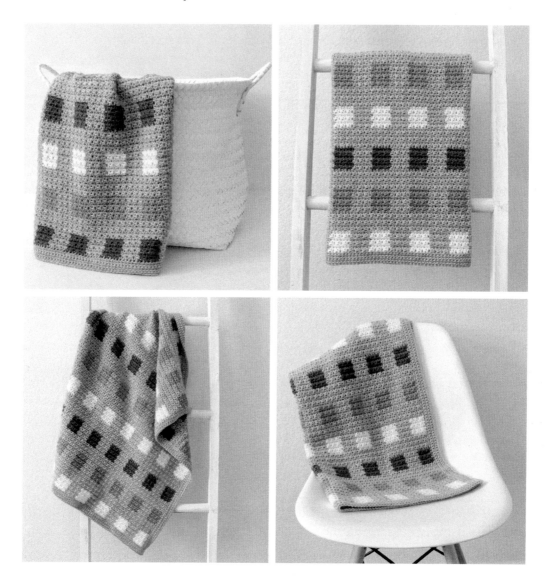

By Hannah

MATERIALS

YARN   Paton's Canadiana
(100% Acrylic, 100 g / 3.5 oz, 187 m / 205 yds)
4 skeins Pale Gray Mix
1 skein White
1 skein Medium Teal
1 skein Teal Heather

HOOK   Size H, 5.00mm hook

TOOLS   Tapestry needle, Scissors

SIZE   Finished size: 30 in x 30 in
Gauge: 4 in = 16 stitches and 12 rows

STITCHES

SINGLE CROCHET (SC): Insert your hook, yarn over (YO) and pull up a loop, YO and pull through both loops on your hook.

HALF DOUBLE CROCHET (HDC): YO, insert your hook, YO and pull up a loop, YO, pull through three loops.

PATTERN

CHAIN 103 with Gray. (Pattern repeat is any odd number multiplied by 6, plus 1.)

ROW 1: Starting in the 2nd chain from the hook, work 1 SC in each chain. On the last stitch, pull through with Teal Heather; do not cut Gray.

ROWS 2 - 7: In the 1st stitch from the hook, *with Teal Heather, work 1 SC. In the next stitch work 1 HDC, carrying the Gray with you along the row as you work. Continue alternating SC, HDC until you have 6 stitches worked. On the 6th stitch, (the last HDC), pull through with Gray before you finish the stitch. Now work the next 6 stitches in Gray, continuing to alternate SC, HDC, and carrying the Teal Heather along as you work. On the last HDC, pull through with Teal Heather. Repeat from * to the end of the row.

When you reach the end of the row, CH 1 and turn. You should end with one HDC in Teal Heather, and when you turn to the next row, wrap the gray yarn around the back of your work and continue to carry it and work over it along the row.

Tip: Each row should start with a SC and end with a HDC, so you are always working a SC into a HDC of the row below and a HDC into a SC of the row below. Always chain 1 and turn at the end of each row.

At the end of row 7, pull through with Gray on the last stitch, and cut the Teal Heather, leaving a tail long enough to weave in later.

ROWS 8 - 13: Work 6 rows of alternating SC and HDC in Gray. CH 1 and turn at the end of each row.

At the end of row 13, pull through with Medium Teal, then CH 1 and turn and carry the Gray around the back of your work.

ROWS 14 - 19: Repeat rows 2 - 7, using Medium Teal and Gray.

ROWS 20 - 25: Repeat rows 8 - 13. On the last stitch of row 25, pull through with White, then chain one and turn and carry the Gray yarn around the back of your work.

ROWS 26 - 31: Repeat rows 2 - 7, using White and Gray.

ROWS 32 - 37: Repeat rows 8 - 13. On the last stitch of row 37, pull through with Teal Heather.

REPEAT ROWS 2 - 37 for the remainder of the blanket, until you reach your desired length and end with a row of White blocks. I ended up repeating the sequence two more times, so that I ended up with three sets of rows of color.

When you reach your desired length, work 1 row of SC with Gray to match row 1 on the other end of the blanket.

BORDER

After I wove in my ends with a tapestry needle, I added a simple single crochet border around the edge with Gray. To do this, pull up a loop in any corner and CH 1. *Then SC around the entire blanket, working 3 SCs into each of the corners. When you reach the corner you started with, slip stitch into the corner and chain 1 and turn.

Repeat from * four more times, or until you reach your desired border thickness.

STRIPES AND DOTS BABY BLANKET

By Haley

MATERIALS

YARN   Caron Simply Soft
(100% acrylic, 170 g/6 oz, 288 m/315 yds)
2 skeins Victorian Rose
2 skeins Gray Heather
2 skeins White

HOOK   Size H, 5.00mm hook

TOOLS   Tapestry needle, Scissors

SIZE   Finished size: 32 in x 32 in
Gauge: 4 in = 14 stitches and 14 rows

STITCHES

WIDE HALF DOUBLE CROCHET (WHDC): Yarn over (YO), insert your hook in between the stitches of the row below (under all 3 loops of stitch), YO and pull up a loop, YO, pull through all 3 loops on hook.

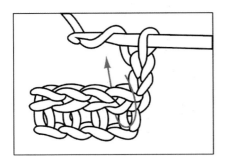

HDC 4 TOGETHER (HDC4TOG) CLUSTER: *YO, insert hook, YO and pull up a loop, repeat from * 3 more times into same space. YO and pull through all loops on your hook.

PATTERN

CHAIN 110 with Grey Heather. (You may chain any number if you'd like to make a larger blanket.)

ROW 1: HDC in the 3rd chain from the hook. HDC in each chain across the row. CH 2 and turn.

ROW 2: WHDC in each space between the stitches across the row, ending the last stitch between the last stitch and the turning chain. CH 2 and turn.

ROWS 3 - 4: Repeat the instructions for row 2. On the last step of the HDC stitch in row 4, lay Victorian Rose across the hook and pull through to change colors.

ROWS 5 - 8: Repeat the instructions for row 2. On the last step of the HDC Stitch in Row 8, lay Gray Heather across the hook and pull through to change colors.

REPEAT CHANGING COLORS EVERY 4 ROWS until your blanket measures approximately 32 inches in length. Tie off and weave in all the ends before starting the border.

BORDER

TOP END: With Victorian Rose, pull up a loop and CH 2 in the last space before the turning chain, (as if you were chaining and turning to continue making the blanket.) Work 1 HDC into that space. Work WHDC in each space across the row. When reaching the end of the row, work 3 HDC around the turning chain.

SIDE ONE: Continue working HDC down the side of the blanket by working one HDC at the end of each row. Work 3 HDC into the bottom corner.

BOTTOM END: Work WHDC in between each stitch across the bottom of the blanket. Work 3 HDC into the corner space.

SIDE TWO: Continue working HDC up the side of the blanket by working one HDC at the end of each row. Join with a slip stitch to starting ch 2 after working one HDC into the corner. CH 2 and turn.

ROUND 2: Work WHDC into each space between the stitches around the blanket. When working around the corners, work 2 HDC in between the first and second stitches, and 2 HDC in between the second and third stitches. Join with a slip stitch to the chain 2 turning chain after working the final 2 HDC between the stitches that make the corner. CH 2 and turn.

ROUND 3: Work WHDC into each space between the stitches. When working the corners, work 3 HDC in the space between the 2 sets of HDC pairs from the row below. (Still work 1 HDC in between the pair of stitches on either side.) Join with a slip stitch to the chain 2 turning chain. CH 2 and turn.

ROUND 4: Repeat round 2 instructions.

ROUND 5 POLKA DOTS: *Slip Stitch in each of the next 6 stitches. CH 3. Work 1 HDC4TOG Cluster in the first chain of the CH 3. Slip stitch into last stitch slip stitched into. Repeat from * around entire blanket. Join with a slip stitch at the end of the round, tie off and weave in the ends.

DIAMOND BOBBLE BABY BLANKET

By Tiffany

MATERIALS

YARN   Red Heart Dreamy
(100% acrylic, 250 g/8.8 oz, 426 m/466 yds)
2 skeins Ivory

HOOK   Size K, 6.50mm hook

TOOLS   Tapestry needle, Scissors

SIZE   Finished size 30 in x 40 in
Gauge: 4 in = 16 stitches and 8 rows

STITCHES

SINGLE CROCHET (SC): Insert your hook, yarn over (YO) and pull up a loop, YO and pull through both loops on your hook.

HERRINGBONE HALF DOUBLE CROCHET (HHDC): YO, insert your hook, YO and pull back through stitch AND through first loop on hook, YO and pull through both remaining loops on the hook.

DOUBLE CROCHET 4 TOGETHER (DC4TOG) BOBBLE: YO, insert your hook, YO, pull up a loop, YO and pull through 2 loops. Then, *YO again, insert your hook into the same space, YO, pull up a loop, YO and pull through 2 loops. Repeat from * 2 more times until you have 5 loops on your hook. Then YO and pull through all 5 loops on your hook.

PATTERN

CHAIN 80. (Pattern repeat is any odd number multiplied by 16.)

ROW 1: In the 2nd chain from the hook, work 1 HHDC. Work 1 HHDC in each of the chains across the row. (79)

ROW 2: CH 1 and turn. Work 1 HHDC in each of the next 15 stitches. *DC4tog bobble in the next stitch. Work 1 SC into the next stitch. Work 1 HHDC in each of the next 14 stitches. Repeat from * across the row.

ROW 3: CH 1 and turn. Repeat row 1.

ROW 4: CH 1 and turn. Work 1 HHDC in each of the next 14 stitches. *DC4tog bobble in the next stitch. Work 1 SC into the next stitch. DC4tog bobble in the next stitch. Work 1 SC into the next stitch. Work HHDC in each of the next 12 stitches. Repeat from * across the row.

ROW 5: CH 1 and turn. Repeat row 1.

ROW 6: CH 1 and turn. Work 1 HHDC in each of the next 13 stitches. *DC4tog bobble in the next stitch. Work 1 SC into the next stitch. DC4tog bobble in the next stitch. Work 1 SC into the next stitch. DC4tog bobble in the next stitch. 1 SC in the next stitch. HHDC in each of the next 10 stitches. Repeat from * across the row.

ROW 7: CH 1 and turn. Repeat row 1.

ROW 8: Repeat row 4.

ROW 9: CH 1 and turn. Repeat row 1.

ROW 10: Repeat row 2.

ROW 11: CH 1 and turn. Repeat row 1.

ROW 12: CH 1 and turn. HHDC in each of the next 7 stitches. *DC4tog bobble in the next stitch. SC in the next stitch. HHDC in each of the next 14 stitches. Repeat from * across the row. (You should end with 1 SC and 6 HHDC after the last bobble of the row.)

ROW 13: CH 1 and turn. Repeat row 1.

ROW 14: CH 1 and turn HHDC in each of the next 6 stitches. *DC4tog bobble in the next stitch. SC in the next stitch. DC4tog bobble in the next stitch. SC in the next. HHDC in each of the next 12 stitches. Repeat from * to the end of the row.

ROW 15: CH 1 and turn. Repeat row 1.

ROW 16: CH 1 and turn. HHDC in each of the next 5 stitches. *DC4tog bobble in the next stitch. SC in the next stitch. DC4tog bobble in the next stitch. SC in the next. DC4tog bobble in the next stitch. SC in the next stitch. HHDC in each of the next 10 stitches. Repeat from * to the end of the row.

ROW 17: CH 1 and turn. Repeat row 1.

ROW 18: Repeat row 14.

ROW 19: CH 1 and turn. Repeat row 1.

ROW 20: Repeat row 12.

ROW 21: CH 1 and turn. Repeat row 1.

ROW 22: To the end of the blanket: Repeat rows 2 through 21 three times.

TASSELS

Cut approximately 11 inch yarn pieces. (You will need lots.) Use 2 strands together to fold in half and feed through the top loops of each stitch. Then open the loop and pull the tails through to secure.

You can choose to cut the ends to even them out after they are all attached.

I found working with Red Heart Dreamy that the blanket did not need blocking. You can wash the blanket in a laundry bag on gentle, then lay the blanket flat to dry.

MODERN GRANNY BABY BLANKET

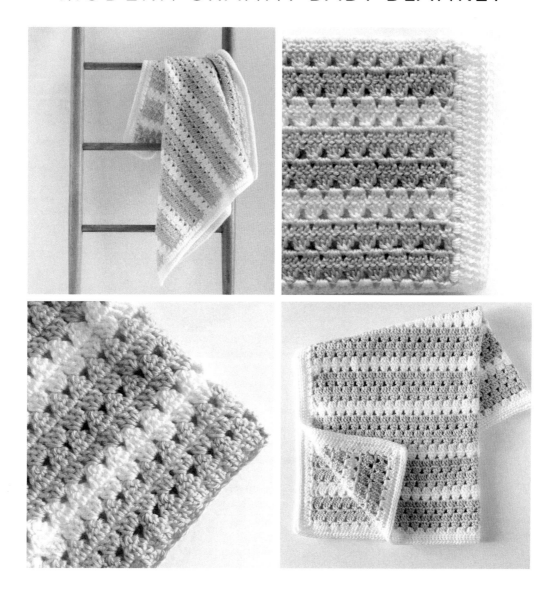

By Tiffany

MATERIALS

YARN   Caron Simply Soft
(100% acrylic, 170 g/6 oz, 288 m/315 yds)
1 skein White
1 skein Soft Blue
1 skein Light Country Peach

HOOK   Size H, 5.00mm hook

TOOLS   Tapestry needle, Scissors

SIZE   Finished size: 30 in x 30 in
Gauge: 4 in = 14 stitches and 7 rows

STITCHES

SINGLE CROCHET (SC): Insert your hook, yarn over (YO) and pull up a loop, YO and pull through both loops on your hook.

DOUBLE CROCHET (DC): YO, insert your hook, YO and pull up a loop, YO, pull through two loops, YO, pull through two remaining loops.

DOUBLE CROCHET 3 TOGETHER (DC3TOG): YO, insert your hook into designated stitch, YO and pull up a loop, YO, pull through two loops, YO, insert your hook into next stitch, then YO and pull up a loop, YO, pull through two loops, YO, insert your hook into next stitch, then YO and pull up a loop, YO, pull through two loops, YO and pull through all loops on hook.

PATTERN

CHAIN 109 with Soft Blue. (Pattern repeat is a multiple of 3, plus 1.)

ROW 1: 1 DC into 4th chain from hook, *SK next 2 chains, 3 DC into next chain. Repeat from * ending with 1 DC into the last chain. CH 3 and turn.

ROW 2: CH 3, 1 DC into first DC (the last DC you made in the row below), *CH 2, DC3TOG the next 3 DC repeat from * ending last repeat with CH 2, DC into next DC, 1 DC into top of beginning 3 chains. Before finishing the last DC of the row, pull through with the new color.

Tip: You should have 34 blocks of triangles plus 2 sets of DC on each end. Take the time to count them—it will help you down the road with keeping the sides of your blanket straight.

CHANGE COLORS (Soft Peach)

ROW 3: CH 3, 3 DC in the chain 2 space between the last DC3TOG and 2 DC of previous row, *3 DC into next chain 2 space, repeat from * ending with 1 DC in top of 3rd chain of turning chain, turn.

ROW 4: CH 4, (counts as 1 DC and 1 CH), *DC3TOG in top of each 3 DC of previous row, CH 2, repeat from * across and end with CH 1, DC into top of chain 3 turning chain, turn. *(35 triangles and 1 DC on each end of the row)*

CHANGE COLORS (White)

ROW 5: CH 3, 1 DC into first DC (the last DC you made from the row below,) *3 DC in next chain 2 space, repeat from * across ending with 2 DC into 3rd chain of CH 4, turn.

ROW 6: CH 3, 1 DC into the next DC (the chain 3 counts as the first stitch, work into the next DC) *CH 2, DC3TOG across the next 3 DC, repeat from * ending last repeat with CH 2, DC into next DC, 1 DC into top of turning chain of chain 3, turn.

REPEAT ROWS 3 - 6 until blanket reaches appx. 30 inches in length, alternating every two rows between Soft Blue, Soft Peach and White.

BORDER

On the last row of the blanket that was worked in White, I did not finish the top half of the triangle. Instead I kept going around the blanket by working 2 DC into the corner and then 2 DC into the side of the posts. Then when I got to the bottom of the blanket, after working 2 DC for the corner, I worked the regular 3 DC into each stitch.

Again, 2 DC for the corner and then 2 DC up the side. I slip stitched to the start, (which is the last row of white I had worked.) Then I went 3 times around the blanket using a HDC slip stitch into the back loop only. (Yarn over, insert your hook into the back loop, yarn over, pull through all the loops on your hook.) That pretty little braid forms as you go.

NOTES

Since each finished "triangle" (the DC that stack on each other) are nestled in between each other, you will notice that the number of them will be different for each color change.

For example, I did a small swatch to test the pattern and I ended up with 8 "triangles" in one row, then 9 in the next, then back to 8 then back to 9.

What I noticed are the rows that have 8 are also the rows where you have 2 DC and the end of the rows. The rows that had 9 "triangles" only had 1 DC on the end. In this blanket, if you use the base chain of 109, you will have 34 and 35 triangles.

You can also carry the yarn up the sides of the blanket when it comes time to switch colors instead of cutting and weaving in the ends after. I found that if I very carefully brought the yarn up the side, paying attention to not make it too tight or too loose, when I went to make a border, they were covered.

If you'd like to add finishing touches to your blanket, lay it out flat on a towel or foam blocking boards if you have them. Use a spray bottle with water to dampen the blanket. Press the blanket into straight lines, massaging the stitches and adjusting your tension. Pin with straight pins and let it dry.

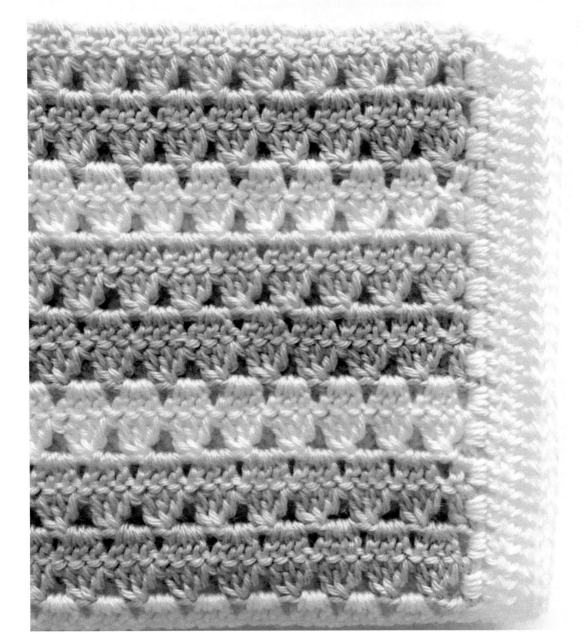

RESOURCES

WEBSITE: Visit daisyfarmcrafts.com for all of our free crochet patterns and be sure to subscribe to our email list!

PINTEREST: Follow us on Pinterest @daisyfarmcrafts to save all your favorite patterns!

FACEBOOK: Follow the Daisy Farm Crafts Facebook page for patterns and videos or join the Daisy Farm Crafters Facebook Group to share pictures, ask pattern questions and meet other crochet friends!

INSTAGRAM: Follow us on Instagram @daisyfarmcrafts to see what we are working on and use #daisyfarmcrafts to share pictures of your finished blankets!

YOUTUBE: Visit the Daisy Farm Crafts YouTube Channel for free crochet video tutorials!

YARN: If the yarn used in one of our patterns is not currently in stock or has been discontinued, visit yarnspirations.com for more yarn options.

We'd like to thank all our crochet friends on Instagram, Facebook, YouTube and Pinterest for using our patterns. We feel your love in every stitch you share with us.

We love to see babies welcomed into the world with a handmade hug.

All our love to you,

Daisy Farm Crafts

Hannah, Nicolina, Tiffany, Haley and Annie

Manufactured by Amazon.ca
Bolton, ON